Kate Chatters, the Great Selbinis, and Lalla Selbini

Brian Chatters

Acknowledgements

The transcribed newspaper articles are from digital images of the original pages, courtesy of the following websites:

- *The British Newspaper Archive (britishnewspaperarchive.co.uk)*
- *Historical American Newspapers (chroniclingamerica.loc.gov)*
- *New York State Historical Photos & Newspapers (www.fultonhistory.com)*
- *Illinois Digital Newspaper Collections (idnc.library.illinois.edu)*
- *Australian Newspaper Archives (trove.nla.gov.au)*

First published 2015

Revised edition 2017

ISBN: 978-1-326-15990-0

Preface

When I began researching my Chatters ancestry in 1998, the sources readily available at that time were restricted to the International Genealogical Index (IGI) published by the Church of Latter Day Saints, the 1881 UK census, and the civil indexes of births, marriages, and deaths, together with the parish registers for a handful of villages in North Essex and South Suffolk, near to the town of Sudbury where my own ancestors came from (the Belchamps, Pentlow, Foxearth, Cavendish, and Glemsford). It soon became apparent that the vast majority of the Chatters families descended from a single source – Henry Chatters who married in 1719. Inevitably, I found a number of records that I could not fit into Henry's family tree. Two marriage records from the IGI were put on the back burner. John Chatters married Mary Dorthy in London in 1831, and Catherine Ann Chatters married William Henry James Knight in Southampton in 1856.

As more information became available on the internet, especially the census returns, I was able to establish that John was indeed descended from Henry Chatters and he was born in Belchamp Otten. Catherine Ann was the daughter of John and Mary. A study of the census returns for the family raised more questions. After 1841, John and Mary were never listed at the same address and, in 1851 Mary's occupation was described as "theatrical". I guessed that John and Mary had separated but I did not have any proof. However, because John was only a distant relative [he is my first cousin, five times removed!], I did not pursue this line of the family history any further until recently. A breakthrough came when a number of newspaper archives became available on the internet. I discovered that Catherine Ann, the daughter of John and Mary, had a stage career under the name of Kate Chatters and I was able to establish a more complete history of the family which is certainly very different from the "ag lab" background of many of my ancestors.

But it was not only Kate who had a show business career. Some of her children and some of her grandchildren were also on the stage and they enjoyed success across the world for many years. The family tree overleaf shows the main descendants of John Chatters.

As with much family history research, a number of questions remain unanswered and some of the evidence is purely circumstantial. However, I hope that my reasoning is sufficiently sound to give credibility to my conclusions.

This book recounts their remarkable story.

Brian Chatters

January 2017

Family tree:

- John Chatters b 1803 d 1873 — m 1831 — Mary Dorthy b c1804 d 1874
  - Mary Chatters b 1838 d 1839
  - John Chatters b 1836 d 1863
  - James Chatters b 1833 d 1854
  - Kate Chatters b 1839 d 1898 — m 1856 — William Knight b 1833 d 1881
    - William Lorenzi b 1868 d 1934 — m 1927 — Bertha Bailey b 1879 d 1945
    - Agnes Knight b 1862 d 1935
    - Lily Knight b 1860 d 1930 — m 1878 — Jack Selbini b 1855 d 1932
      - Mizpah Selbini b 1886 d 1955 — m 1922 — Archie Royer b 1869 d 1956
      - Leola Selbini b 1882 d 1948
      - Lalla Selbini b 1878 d 1942 — m 1902 — Willy Pantzer b 1872 d 1955
        - Barbara Pantzer b 1902 d 1973
      - Victor Selbini b c1881 d 1938
      - Chris'pher McCoy b 1880 d 1881
    - Kate Knight b 1864 d 1952
    - Rosina Knight b 1861 d 1861
    - Catherine Knight b 1858 d 1858
    - James Knight b 1866 d 1866

5

Contents

Part 1:

Kate Chatters

Early Life in London

John Chatters was one of nine children born to Job Chatters (1771 – 1837) and Ann Yeldham (abt 1770 – 1839). He was born in 1803 and he was baptised in Belchamp Otten in the county of Essex on the tenth day of April 1803. John's father had served as an agricultural labourer on the same farm for over forty years but he [John] wanted more out of life and he was determined not to follow in his father's footsteps. As a young man, he moved to London in search of a better life but, like many people at that time, he found life no better than that in his home village.

John met Mary Dorthy[1] in London and they married at the parish church of Saint Dunstan in Stepney on the seventeenth day of October 1831.The census records state that she was born in the parish of Minories in the City of London but a search through the baptisms records from 1790 to 1810 has been fruitless. Her age given on the various census returns differs by nine years giving her date of birth between 1797 and 1806.

At first, John and Mary lived a normal but difficult life in Hackney, typical of working class families of the time. John was unskilled and he worked as a porter, probably in one of the London markets. He and Mary had four children:

- James was born in 1833 and he was baptised in Stepney on the thirtieth day of June 1833.
- John was born in 1836 and he was baptised in Hackney on the twenty-eighth day of February 1836.

---

[1] The marriage certificate records Mary's surname as *Dorthy* but the birth records for their children record it as *Dougherty, Doherty*, or *Dourty*.

- Mary was born in 1838 and she was baptised in Hackney on the twenty-fifth day of February 1838. Sadly, Mary died as an infant in 1839 and she was buried in Hackney on the seventh day of June 1839.
- Catherine Ann (known as Kate) was born in 1839 and she was baptised in Hackney on the fifth day of January 1840.

The family lived firstly in Wick Street in Hackney and in about 1840 they moved to Ridges Place in Bethnal Green, which was situated in John's Street near to Gray's Court. Neither of these addresses was considered a slum so John was probably making an adequate living at the time. When the 1841 census was taken, John was listed with his wife and family in Bethnal Green but he was, in fact, visiting his eldest sister Ann. She was married to Thomas Hookway and they were living at Grays Hall[2] in Thurrock. Also listed at the same address were eight of the children of Thomas and Ann, one of Ann's other brothers, Jeffery who was widowed, two sisters Charlotte and Mary Ann, Mary Ann's husband Charles Tokely, and Charlotte's illegitimate son John Hartford. There is no obvious reason for the large family gathering. Both parents, Job and Ann, had been dead for some time and the family was poor so it is unlikely that they met to discuss any inheritances. Nor were there any family weddings or baptisms at the time. Perhaps they were just a close family who liked to meet together occasionally.

---

[2] Grays Hall was originally the manor house but, by 1841, it had become dilapidated and it was rented out to labourers. The lord of the manor lived in Sherfield House which was about half a mile south of Grays Hall. A "new" Grays Hall was built on the estate in 1869 and the original hall was eventually demolished in 1901.

Kate, the youngest child of John and Mary, was a pretty and talented child but unfortunately this fact was to cause the breakup of the family. Probably driven by her mother, Kate began performing in the music halls between the ages of seven and eight years. She soon began performing as a "clever little danseuse" (ballet dancer) in provincial theatres which were beginning to open across the country. Many of the so-called theatres were little more than a room in an inn that was reserved for entertainment, allowing the customers to eat and drink while being entertained. In 1851, Kate and her mother were listed at the home of William Pearce, a railway porter, in Derby and Mary's occupation was stated to be *theatrical*. It is likely that Mary had rented a room while Kate was performing in a local theatre.

Meanwhile, John remained in London with his two sons and in 1851 he was working as a greengrocer. Son James began working as a lithograph printer but, soon afterwards, he enlisted in the army and he saw active service during the Crimean War at the battle of Balaclava, famous for the charge of the Light Brigade, and at the siege of Sebastopol. Sadly, he died early on in the war on the twentieth day of November 1854, not of injuries received, but of dysentery due to the poor sanitary conditions that the soldiers had to endure, and which Florence Nightingale successfully campaigned against to bring about improvements but, of course, it was too late for James.

John junior joined his mother and sister in Hampshire and John senior was left on his own. In the 1861 census, John senior was listed as a visitor at the home of his sister Mary and her husband Charles Tokely in Alphamstone in the county of Essex. His occupation was stated to be a stockman. Charles was a farmer so it is likely that he had given John a job on his farm.

His son John settled in Portsmouth and he married during the 1850s to Sarah but I have failed to find a marriage record for them (they may have just lived as man and wife). Sarah died on the seventeenth day of May 1859 of pulmonary tuberculosis (phthisis) at her home, 69 Russell Street, in Portsea. John continued to live in Russell Street and his occupation at the time of the 1861 census was stated to be a "waiter and general dealer". His mother was living with him together with Kate's daughter, Lily. Mary's occupation was stated to be a shopkeeper. John died at home of pneumonia on the eighth day of February 1863 at the age of thirty-seven years.

John senior spent the last years of his life eking out a living the best he could until he was too old and infirm to care for himself. In 1871 and no longer able to work, he was living with his sister Charlotte Brown and her daughter Mary Ann Westwood in Hackney. John was admitted to the Hackney workhouse on the fourteenth day of April 1873 and he died soon afterwards on the eleventh day of July 1873 at the age of seventy years.

After the death of John junior, Mary moved back to London and looked after Kate's children while Kate continued touring the provincial theatres. Mary was listed in Beale Street in Tower Hamlets together with her grandchildren Agnes and William at the time of the 1871 census, but Lily was listed as a visitor at the home of Philip and Hannah Hill in Usher Road which is about five hundred yards from where her grandmother and her siblings were living. The other grandchild, Kate, is not listed but she may have been omitted in error. Mary died on the twelfth day of January 1874, at number thirty-five Lefevre Road in Bow, which was close to Beale Street where she had been living in 1871[3]. The cause of Mary's death was *gangrene of the leg*, and the informant who registered her death was E Jones. He (or she) was possible living at the same address or was a neighbour. On her death certificate, Mary was described as the *widow of John Chatters, coach painter*. It is likely that this information was provided by a close relative, which would have been either her daughter Kate or one of her grandchildren.

---

[3] It was not unusual for people living in rented accommodation to move home quite often. According to Charles Booth's survey of London's poverty, the area where Mary lived was classified as mainly poor with a few roads classified as mixed (some poor, some comfortable).

Kate's Career Takes Off

While John was being neglected by his family, Kate's career went from strength to strength. She joined the company at Rendle's Concert Hall in Portsea on Boxing Day, 1853 and established her base in Portsmouth, initially living with her mother and brother. In 1856, she joined the company of artistes at the Albion Music Hall, located at the Blue Boar Tavern in East Street, Southampton. There she developed her act where she was described as a *characteristic singer and clog, patten, and slipper dancer*. Her speciality was to perform a hornpipe in pattens[4] on slabs, which was well received by the public. As a characteristic singer, Kate sang songs portraying an individual or character type, interspersed with comic patter or chat with the audience.

It was about this time that Kate met William James Henry Knight and they married at All Saints parish church, Southampton on the fifteenth day of May 1856 when Kate was just sixteen years old. William was born in 1833 in Southampton and he was baptised in Holyrood on the twenty-second day of September 1833, the son of William Knight, a mariner, and his wife Elizabeth.

At the end of 1857, Kate appeared as the star attraction at William's City Concert Hall in Bristol where she was billed as *the eminent comic characteristic singer and dancer from the London concerts* although I do not believe that she had appeared in London by that time. She remained in Bristol for

---

[4] Pattens were wooden clogs worn over normal shoes in order to raise the feet above the mud and the dirt of the streets.

about ten weeks and she quickly gained favour with the audiences:

The pretty Miss Kate Chatters has been the chief celebrity of the Christmas week, and has been eminently successful in hitting the taste of her audience. Her "drum song" in particular produces quite a furore.

While in Bristol, Kate gave birth to her first child, Catherine Mary, who sadly died after a few months.

Kate returned to perform with the Albion Music Hall company in Southampton after she had appeared in Bristol and, in 1859, she performed in Northampton, Great Bridge (Staffordshire), and West Bromwich, but she then had to put her show business career on hold when she became pregnant with her second child, Lily, who was born in Portsea in 1860. Soon after her confinement, Kate advertised for new engagements. Her husband, William, was a gilder by trade but I believe that he entered show business as a comic singer[5] in order to support his new wife in her career. At the end of the year, William and Kate appeared on the same bill at the Royal Arms Music Hall in Aldershot. In February 1861, they joined the *Proprietors and Professionals Mutual Anti-Agency Society*. The society had been formed to enable talented

---

[5] The evidence to support the claim that William was also in show business is purely circumstantial. The name "W Knight" appears on the same bill as Kate on a number of occasions so I have concluded that he is Kate's husband. I have failed to find William or Kate in the 1861 census and they may have been performing in Ireland. However, an added confusion is that William's occupation was recorded as "gilder and carver" on the baptism record for daughter Rosina. If he had continued working as a gilder whilst Kate was on tour rather than touring with her, why is he not residing with his mother-in-law, Mary Chatters, and his daughter Lily in Southampton?

artistes of proven ability to obtain engagements and to prevent incompetent artistes being forced upon proprietors by unprincipled agents. A few months earlier, Kate had been approached to join the Lowick's Musical Agency. Whether the agency was "unprincipled" or not is a matter of conjecture.

Kate's return to the stage was short-lived. She gave birth to a second daughter, Rosina George Knight, in the summer of 1861 at North Cross Street in Gosport. Sadly, her daughter did not survive. Rosina was privately baptised on the sixth day of July and she died soon afterwards at the age of three weeks. She was buried in Ann's Hill Cemetery in Gosport on the twelfth day of July.

William and Kate returned to the stage a few months later and they undertook an engagement at Connell's Saloon in Dublin from October to December 1861 where they were well-received:

Miss Kate Chatters made her first appearance this week. Her singing and dancing are regularly encored. The performance of a hornpipe in pattens on a slab is hailed with intense applause. Mr W Knight's effusions in the comic line are highly successful.

William and Kate continued to perform on and off for the next three years; appearing in Manchester, Glasgow, Birkenhead, Liverpool, and Portsmouth. Kate had two more daughters, Kate and Agnes, during that period. Her career was in the ascendency and she was in great demand although, due to her domestic life, Kate was unable to fulfil all the offers of engagements that she had received. In April 1864 and soon after the birth of her fourth daughter, she suffered from a severe bout of rheumatism which confined her to her bed and she was forced to cancel a number of engagements. Kate and William had their three surviving daughters baptised at the parish church of St Luke in Southampton on the twelfth day of February 1865. The baptism records state that William's trade was a gilder although he may still have been performing on the stage. However, he failed to make a successful career in show business.

Leaving her mother, Mary Chatters, to care for the children, Kate was now in a position to dedicate all her time to her career. She placed an advertisement in *The Era* trade magazine announcing her availability:

Miss Kate Chatters (the original) characteristic vocalist and danseuse, begs to inform managers of first-class concert halls that she is at liberty to make arrangements for future dates. Good wardrobe, good appearance, and a great variety of new songs, dances, etc. First class references, "I have much pleasure in recommending Miss Kate Chatters as a Serio-Comic and characteristic vocalist and dancer. I consider her exceedingly clever. She has fulfilled an engagement of some weeks at the Music Hall, Southampton, to the entire satisfaction of both audience and myself, receiving always a fourth and fifth call at each turn" (JW GORDON, Music Hall, Southampton)

Kate soon received several bookings that kept her fully occupied throughout 1865, appearing in Nottingham, Wolverhampton, Birmingham, and Leicester. Kate made her London debut with the company of Wilton's Magnificent

Music Hall in Whitechapel in July 1865. She was obviously successful and popular with the public as she remained with the company for over three months. However, the pay was probably quite low because Kate also appeared at the Knightsbridge Music Hall at the same time in order to boost her earnings. She remained in the capital until the end of the year.

While in London, Kate gave birth to her first son, James, but, like two of his sisters, he too died in infancy.

Kate toured almost non-stop for the next eight years but, in 1868, her schedule was further interrupted when she gave birth in Liverpool to another son, William John. She performed mainly in the north of England[6], and she became a firm favourite in Liverpool, appearing there on several occasions.

In addition to her trademark clog dancing, Kate occasionally appeared in novelty ballets such as *The Village in an Uproar* (in Leicester), *The Greek Mythological Ballet* as a character called *Statueska* (in Worcester), and *The Marble Statue* (in Nottingham). Among her characters, *Nobody's Child* and a buxom *Lancashire Lass* were very popular.

She sang many popular songs of the day, now long-forgotten. Among them were *My Love, Dan, is an Irishman*, which was

---

[6] Towns and cities where Kate performed included Ashton-under-Lyme, Belfast, Birkenhead, Birmingham, Blackburn, Bolton, Bradford, Briggale (Yorkshire), Burnley, Burslem, Chester, Dublin, Edinburgh, Glasgow, Gloucester, Halifax, Hanley, Hartlepool, Hull, Leeds, Leicester, Liverpool, Manchester, Middlesbrough, Newcastle-upon-Tyne, Northampton, Poplar, Preston, Sheffield, South Shields, Southwark, Spennymoor, West Bromwich, Wigan, Woolwich, and Worcester.

written by Edward Harley Tannett, who called himself "The Cheshire Poet", *The Drum Song* and *Sailor Boy*.

In early 1870, Kate was inadvertently drawn into a dispute with another act, *Charlie Aldridge and Annie Chatters*.

Rivalry in the Music Halls

At the beginning of 1870, a dispute arose between Annie and Kate Chatters. *The Era* trade magazine reported incorrectly on the sixteenth day of January that "Mr C Aldridge and Miss Kate Chatters (Negro comedians)" had appeared at the Old Tankard Music Hall in Sheffield. Charlie and Annie took offence at the error and issued the following letter which appeared in *The Era* the following week:

Sir, will you permit me, through the medium of your valuable columns, to correct an error concerning Miss Kate Chatters and Miss Annie Chatters, which if allowed to pass unnoticed, may be the cause of great injury to the latter, she being a young and clever artiste, very popular and in good request, whereby the former lady is a middle-aged party, in quite a different line of business, and should her name be coupled with mine, it would be detrimental to us in procuring engagements. Your obedient servants CHARLIE ALDRIDGE and ANNIE (but not Kate) CHATTERS. Old Tankard, Sheffield.

Two responses appeared the week after that:

Sir, my attention has been called to a letter in your paper Sunday last, which, if allowed to pass without notice, might very seriously affect me. If we all thought the same, perhaps contempt would be the best way to deal with such scurrilous attempts to slander. But as I have been a favourite in the profession for twenty years (having commenced my career when between seven and eight years of age), I must inform you, for my own credit's sake, that there is no Miss Annie Chatters in the business, and will not be her case, except by marriage, her name being Edney. I have never seen the lady but once in my life, and then we were not introduced to each other. I beg to subscribe myself your obedient servant; Miss KATE CHATTERS, Museum Concert Hall, Birmingham.

Sir, as a constant subscriber to your valuable paper, I last Saturday, as usual, had my hour or so's enjoyment while perusing its columns, during which time I glanced at the "Original Correspondence" and there saw a letter addressed to you, signed Charles Aldridge and Annie (not Kate) Chatters, which I consider needs a reply. I can fully understand the feeling that prompted the writers to address you on the subject as, whatever our profession or business, we certainly like to have credit for what we do; but I cannot see why a mistake on the part of your Sheffield reporter should be seized as an opportunity not to be missed for insulting publicly Miss Kate Chatters, who most certainly was not to blame. I can come to no other conclusion but that, on some previous occasion, there must have been some disagreement between the parties and Mr C. A., in a noble and manly manner, took it upon himself to address you in his own peculiar style. He mentions the lady in question as "a middle-aged party" and insinuates that, should her name be coupled with his, it would be detrimental to him in procuring engagements. With reference to Miss Kate Chatters being "middle-aged" as stated, not being acquainted with particulars concerning that lady's birth and parentage, I cannot state facts; but judging from her personal appearance, and the exceedingly clever and artistic manner in which she goes through her business, executing some most difficult dances with the greatest of ease – if she is "so aged", all I can say is she is a wonder. After all, I must admit that the remark about age is almost beneath notice; but the insinuations concerning the lady's professional abilities ought to be most emphatically contradicted, as I am sure that every Professional who had had the opportunity of seeing "Miss Kate's" business must acknowledge that she is a lady possessing far more than the average amount of talent, being an excellent burlesque actress, a good singer, and one of the best lady dancers on the Music Hall stage; and I may add, for the edification of Mr C. A., the lady is also an established favourite in London, where, by the by, I cannot remember having the pleasure of seeing him. Should he ever honour London with a visit, which, if reports speak truly, I consider very doubtful, I shall most certainly go and judge of the capabilities of this sensitive gentleman. In conclusion, Mr C. A., although calling attention to the fact that his lady partner is young and clever, makes no allusion to his own age, but from the tone of his letter, I have certainly come to the conclusion that he is "young indeed"; in fact, not yet arrived at the age of discretion. Trusting you will favour me of inserting this, I am Sir, yours respectfully, A FRIEND IN NEED.

Kate, of course, was only thirty years old. Coincidentally, Annie and Kate were both appearing in Birmingham just after the exchange of letters although they were appearing at different venues. Kate was at the London Museum Music Hall and Annie was at the Birmingham Concert Hall.

Annie Chatters

Annie was born Elizabeth Ann Edney in Spitalfields, Whitechapel, in 1845, the daughter of William Edney and his wife Eliza Fernley. She was baptised at the parish church of Saint Leonard in Shoreditch on the fourteenth day of September 1845. At that time, William's occupation was a bookbinder but soon afterwards, he became a professional musician. Eliza died in 1854 and she was buried at the parish church of Saint Mary, Haggerston, on the twenty-third day of April. By 1861, William, who was a vocalist, had joined forces with his daughter, who was then still known as Elizabeth. She was to team up later with Frank Chatters.

In 1864, Frank Chatters, a comic singer, made his debut at Cooper's Music Hall in Leicester. He was described as *a great favourite and is one of the best comic singers yet heard at the establishment* and he was so popular that his contract was extended by a month. Frank was born Edward Richardson in about 1841, the son of John Richardson, a carver and *Chatters* was his stage name.

Nelly Batchelour, a singer, was also appearing at Cooper's Music Hall on the same bill as Frank and they entered into a relationship. Nelly, whose full name was Ellen Catherine Batchelour, was born in about 1846. She was the daughter of Charles Batchelour, a piano tuner, and his wife Mary Farrington, a pianist and singer. A daughter, Nelly Frances Amelia, was born to Frank and Nelly on the twentieth day of April 1865 and she was baptised in St Pancras on the twenty-sixth day of April 1869. Both her birth record and baptism record give her surname as *Chatters*. It may be that Ellen did not know Frank's real name. Nelly married Daniel Cronin in St Pancras on the fifth day of August 1883. Frank's relationship with Nelly Batchelour was brief and they split up about the same time as their daughter was born. Nelly had a successful solo career for the next five years and she then teamed up as a singing duo with Albert White whom she married in 1871.

In 1865, Frank met William and Elizabeth Edney when they appeared on the same bill at the Phoenix Music Hall in Maidstone. They soon teamed up to form the Jordan Minstrels[7] and they made their debut at the Canterbury Hall in Brighton. The act was well received and there was praise for Frank's singing and Elizabeth's dancing:

The Jordan Minstrels make friends, being at present, we think, unknown to fame, but it will not be long before they establish a reputation for Mr Chatters, in addition to his vocal abilities, is a capital dancer and Miss Edney's clog hornpipe is the best we have seen for some time.

Frank and Elizabeth married at the parish church of St George the Martyr in Southwark on the twenty-seventh day of September 1865. Elizabeth's father, William, married Eliza Sandalls at the same time. William was forty-two years old; Eliza was eighteen years old.

The minstrel act was short-lived and Frank had returned to his solo career by the summer of 1865. He remained busy throughout the remainder of the year with month long

---

[7] Just before they called themselves the "Jordan Minstrels", Frank, William, and Elizabeth had been performing on the same bill as an act known as the "Royal Jordan Minstrels" who had been in show business for many years.

engagements in Ramsgate, Dover, and Maidstone, and he finished with an appearance at Odd Fellow's in Ipswich. He continued to receive good reviews.

In December 1865, Frank teamed up again with Elizabeth who had adopted the stage name of *Annie Chatters*. They developed a Negro act, such acts being very popular at the time, and described themselves as "American Comedians" although they were both British. It was quite common at the time for artistes (or the theatre managers) to assume whatever nationality had the most appeal to the audiences. Frank and Annie spent most of 1866 touring the rapidly expanding towns in the north of England. They appeared in Sheffield, Newcastle-upon-Tyne, Leeds, Manchester, Brownhills, Sunderland, Bolton, Blackburn, Huddersfield, Ashton-under-Lyme, and Rochdale. They also undertook an engagement in Glasgow. For a short time, Frank and Annie teamed up with Andy Whiteley and they continued to perform their Negro act.

Frank and Annie made their London debut in May 1867 by joining the company of Wilton's Music Hall, the same place where Kate Chatters had appeared two years earlier and Andy Whiteley had been replaced by two new members of the troupe; Will Parr and Little Pete. Annie was described as "the only American clog, boot and pump dancer in England"! By the end of 1867, Frank and Annie appeared in Ashton-under-Lyme by which time Will Parr and Little Pete had been replaced by a young Minnie Nott.

Frank's career was cut short when he developed laryngitis at the end of 1867. He may have contracted the disease by straining his voice on stage. He continued performing for some months which probably aggravated the condition and he probably made his last appearance with Annie in Bury on the tenth day of May 1868[8]. Frank died in London of *phthisis laryngitis* at the age of twenty-seven years on the nineteenth day of October 1868. Annie continued with her show business career and she teamed up with Minnie Nott as duettists and dancers. The act was short lived and Annie then teamed up with Charlie Aldridge who was described as a Negro vocalist and instrumentalist. Annie would have seen Charlie as a natural replacement for Frank so that she could resume the minstrel act. The partnership was a success and the couple appeared at numerous music halls throughout 1869. They appeared in Grimsby, Bolton, Leicester, Rochdale, Glasgow, Aberdeen, Birmingham, Sunderland, and Bradford.

In spite of their concerns about future engagements in the dispute over Annie being mistaken for Kate, Charlie and Annie continued to have regular bookings for a number of further years although they did not always perform together as an act. When they appeared together in London in 1872, Annie was billed as the "champion lady dancer of the world". In 1877, they appeared at Collin's Concert Hall in Islington as duettists and, in 1880, they were booked to appear at the Theatre Royal in Plymouth together with "infant Annie". Had Charlie and Annie had a child?

Meanwhile, Kate continued with her career.

---

[8] The appearance in Bury was the last one to be reported in the newspapers. Frank and Annie may have performed after this date although it must have been extremely painful for Frank to continue with his act.

Scandal

At the end of 1870, Kate returned to Belfast at St Patrick's Music Hall where she starred as the leading character in a pantomime called *"Rory O'More, the genius of Erin and the magic harp"*. The pantomime ran for nine weeks and Kate was praised for her dancing and vivacious acting which won "golden opinions from all sorts of people". She returned to Belfast at the end of 1871 and again in 1872. For reasons which are not clear, Kate re-launched her career under the name of *Hilda* and she appeared in Huddersfield in April 1873. However, she suffered a "severe indisposition" which put her out of action for most of that year but in December she announced (under the name of Hilda) that she was available again for engagements:

Hilda (late K Chatters), the legitimate serio and characteristic vocalist, burlesque actress, and dancer, tenders her thanks to proprietors for their enquiries during her severe indisposition, and begs to inform them she has once more resumed her profession with a choice selection of songs and a first-class wardrobe. Not a champion, but acknowledged by the profession and the press to be one of the prettiest clog and pump dancers extant. Now fulfilling third successful engagement at the Alhambra, South Shields. To follow in 1874, Lancaster six nights, Alhambra Liverpool twelve nights, Princess's Leeds three weeks, Day's Birmingham three weeks, Mechanic's Hull twelve nights, Alhambra Bradford six nights, Wear Sunderland twelve nights. At liberty May 4th, 11th, and 18th for two weeks.

It was about this time that Kate began her relationship with Henry Flowerday. Henry was a master mariner who was married at the time to Caroline Jane Thornton. The "severe disposition" was the fact that Kate was carrying Henry's baby!

Henry Flowerday was born on the twenty-second day of February 1836[9] and he was baptised in Greenwich on the thirty-first day of July, the son of Francis William Flowerday and Ann Starkey. Henry was born into a seafaring family. His grandfather, Francis Flowerday, was born in Stalham in the county of Norfolk in 1774 and he had a career in the Royal Navy, serving on *HMS Monmouth*, *HMS Stately*, and *HMS Illustrious*. This last ship was part of the fleet that captured Mauritius in December 1810 during the Napoleonic War. Francis was discharged from the ship on the twenty-second day of December to Bourbon Hospital in Mauritius where, it is believed, he died although his name continued on the muster list for HMS Illustrious up to 1814. His two sons, Henry's father, Francis William Flowerday, and his uncle Joshua, were admitted to the Greenwich Hospital School on the seventh day of July 1809. The school had been established in 1694 to provide assistance and education for the children of seafarers of the Royal and Merchant Navies who had been either slain or disabled. The boys at the school were committed to entering the naval service. The father of Francis and Joshua was still alive at the time they entered the school

---

[9] Henry's Masters Certificate, which was issued in 1876, states that he was born in 1832 although the year is questionable. It is unlikely that he was born in that year as his brother would only have been five months old. The year of birth of 1836 is consistent with his age given on his death record and on the census returns. 1836 is also the year in which Henry was baptised.

and he was serving on HMS Illustrious so it is likely that he had been severely injured which is perhaps why he was discharged to Bourbon Hospital in Mauritius the following year. Francis, Henry's father, was stated to be a fisherman at the time of the baptisms of his children. Of course, he may have served in the navy before becoming a fisherman as he was about thirty-four years old when his eldest child was born. According to unverified information from the internet, Francis died of mumps on the fourth day of April 1839 on board the vessel "William and Mary" in the North Sea. There were a number of vessels bearing the name "William and Mary" at that time.

Francis' oldest son, Francis William, was admitted to the Greenwich Hospital School on the twenty-fifth day of August 1843 at the age of twelve years but Henry was possibly too young at that time. However, he entered the Merchant Navy in about 1850 and served on the vessel the "Prince of Wales" as an assistant steward but after about five months he joined the "North Star" and then the "Light of the Age" until 1858 where he rose through the ranks to Quartermaster. I believe that these three vessels were large passenger ships travelling between England and Australia. Henry married Caroline Jane Thornton in Woolwich on the twelfth day of May 1857 between voyages to Australia.

After 1858, Henry made a major change in his navy career by joining the crew of the "Jane Maria" as mate. The ship was a brigantine, carrying cargo between Newcastle-upon-Tyne and London (possibly coal!). Henry's family lived in Greenwich and he had six children by Caroline. He was appointed Master of the "Jane Maria" on the first day of January 1868 and his regular trips between Newcastle and London gave him the opportunity to start an affair with Kate without his wife's knowledge. It is possible that Kate was unaware of the fact that Henry was married at the start of their relationship.

Kate gave birth to a daughter, Jane Maria Flowerday (named after Henry's ship), on the twenty-third day of October 1873 in South Shields in the county of Durham[10]. Jane was adopted by William and Mary Gilmore but it is unclear whether Jane was aware of her birth parents until she was an adult. When she married in 1893, her marriage certificate recorded her name as Jane Maria Gilroy, daughter of William Gilroy. Her husband, Thomas Ward Huggitt, died in a shipping accident in 1906 and she applied for a copy of her birth certificate in 1907, possibly needed to claim compensation from the shipping company. The birth certificate confirmed Jane's natural parents.

Kate made a number of appearances throughout 1874, performing in Liverpool, Leeds, Birmingham, Bradford, Newcastle-upon-Tyne and Sunderland but I have found no further information on any engagements after that time, so she probably retired from the stage. Her last appearance was at the Northumberland Music Hall in North Shields. Throughout 1874, she had reverted to her original stage name of *Kate Chatters*.

Kate made South Shields her home but Henry continued to liaise with his wife. His occupation as a mariner and his regular trips between Newcastle and London gave him the

---

[10] Jane Maria was known as Jeannie and she was baptised in St Hilda, South Shields, on the fourth day of January 1874.

perfect excuse to cheat on both Caroline and Kate. Caroline gave birth to their youngest child, a daughter Edith whose birth was registered in Greenwich between April and June 1874.

Kate was pregnant again by Henry in 1875. A son, John Hedley Flowerday, was born on the twenty-eighth day of July 1875 in South Shields[11]. I have no further information on John who was also possibly adopted. Kate and Henry had a third child, a daughter Elizabeth Mary Flowerday, whose birth was registered in South Shields between July and September 1876. Like her two siblings, Elizabeth was also adopted. Her adopted parents were William and Elizabeth Wilkinson.

Henry received his Master's Certificate on the nineteenth day of October 1876 at Sunderland while still Master of the "Jane Maria". However, according to the 1881 census, Kate and Henry were living together as man and wife and they were listed on board the vessel the "Tennessee of Newcastle" which was berthed at Chatham Dockyard. The ship was a 269-ton barque (a deep water cargo carrier) used for home and coastal trade. Henry's wife Caroline was living in Lewisham with four of her children. She was stated to be married (mariner's wife) so it is still unclear whether she knew about Henry's liaison with Kate although it is likely that she did know by that time. There were no more children born to Henry and Caroline after Edith who, according to the 1881 census, was "afflicted from birth". Kate was now travelling with Henry so he did not appear to be making any effort to keep his two families apart. Henry changed ships again in

---

[11] John Hedley was baptised in St Hilda, South Shields, on the tenth day of October 1875.

1881 and he joined the vessel the "Sherbo" as First Mate. The "Sherbo" was built in 1880 and belonged to the Somerset and Dorset fleet. It was their largest ship at 239 tons (but smaller than the "Tennessee") and it was used to ferry passengers from Burnham-on-Sea. It also carried livestock and cargo. Why Henry decided to move to a smaller ship in a lesser position (First Mate rather than Master) can only be speculated upon. Perhaps he had had enough of hauling coal!

Kate's husband William Knight had died in 1881 and Henry's wife Caroline died in 1884, her death being registered in Maidstone between July and September. The deaths of their spouses allowed Kate and Henry to marry and this they did at All Saints church, Poplar, on the twenty-seventh day of April, 1885. The marriage certificate stated that her father, John, was a coach builder but, of course, the statement was untrue. It was not unusual for people to fabricate such details on their marriage records if they wished to hide their past.

At the time of the 1891 census, Kate was listed as a married woman living in Oak Tree Cottage at Wanstead in the county of Essex. Henry was not listed at home but he may have been on a ship. Perhaps more surprisingly given Kate's past relationships with her children, Henry and Caroline's youngest daughter Edith was living with her following Caroline's death. She was stated to be "deformed" so it is obvious that she suffered from a physical disability. However, the disability did not stop Edith from leading a normal life and she subsequently married and went on to have children.

Kate had a very successful stage career for over twenty-five years. However, her relationship with her parents suffered as a consequence. As previously stated, her father died a pauper in the Hackney workhouse and her mother Mary was left to raise her children. Kate separated from her husband William Knight some time before 1873 when she started the liaison with Henry Flowerday. William was listed in the 1881 census as living in the Southampton workhouse. He died soon afterwards at the age of forty-eight years and his death was registered in Southampton between July and September 1881.

Kate died on the sixth day of February 1898 when she was fifty-eight years old. The following announcement appeared in the newspaper:

DEATHS. FLOWERDAY – Feb 6th, at her residence at Leytonstone, after a protracted illness, Mrs Flowerday (Kate Chatters), mother of Lilly Selbini, of the Selbini Troupe, and Will Lorenzo, of Phillips and Lorenzo[12] Troupe. Deeply mourned by her sorrowing relatives and friends.

Although the death notice does not mention Kate's husband, Henry, or her other children, the family had remained in contact with each other. When Kate's granddaughter, Lalla Selbini, married in 1902, her guests at the wedding included her maternal aunts Kate and Agnes and her adopted grandfather, Henry Flowerday (see later).

Henry remarried soon after Kate's death to Emma Sarah Porter; according to the marriage record, he was sixty-two years old and she was twenty-three years old [in fact, she was only twenty-one years old!]. The marriage took place in Canning Town, West Ham on the thirty-first day of August

---

[12] "Lorenzo" is incorrect – the act was known as the "Sisters Phillips and Brothers Lorenzi".

1898. Emma had given birth to a son, Henry, by Henry two years earlier when Kate was still alive! Just like the fact that Henry had cheated on his first wife Caroline with Kate, he now cheated on Kate with Emma. Henry and Emma had further children; Beatrice born in 1899, Victor Edward born in 1902, and Lalla Frances born in 1904. Henry died in West Ham on the thirtieth day of June 1907. His estate was valued at just £96 10s. His widow, Emma, married again in 1908 to Ernest Wiley, a milkman. They had four further children; Ernest born in 1909, Jessie born in 1912, Dorothy born in 1914, and Lily born in 1917.

So, what happened to Kate's surviving children by William Knight? Following her mother's death, Kate needed to make arrangements for the care of her children. Lily, the eldest daughter, was fourteen years old and she was able to begin her own career in show business. The other children were probably adopted or fostered.

Kate's Children

Lily Knight

Lily in 1894(Source: The Sketch, October   17, 1894)

Lily Knight was born on the fifteenth day of January 1860 in Russell Street, Portsea Island. She was baptised on the twelfth day of February 1865 at St Luke's church in Southampton, together with her sisters Kate and Agnes. Lily was living with her grandmother, Mary, and her uncle, John Chatters, in Portsea at the time of the 1861 census. She married Patrick Joseph McCoy in 1878 and the marriage was registered in Southampton between April and June. Patrick and Lily went on to form the world famous trick cycle act, *The Selbinis* (more on this story later).

Agnes Knight

Agnes was born in 1862 and her birth was registered in Liverpool between July and September. She was baptised at St Luke's church in Southampton on the twelfth day of February 1865 together with her sisters, Lily and Kate. Like her siblings, Agnes was possibly adopted after her grandmother died in 1874[13]. She married Samuel Ottaway in Leytonstone, Essex, on the twenty-ninth day of July 1886. Samuel was born in Maidstone on the third day of January 1861 and he was a licensed victualler. Samuel and Agnes did not have any children and they lived in Southampton. Agnes died at home on the twenty-sixth day of December 1935 at the age of seventy-three years. Samuel died in the Borough Hospital, Southampton, on the twenty-fourth day of January 1944 at the age of eighty-three years. Patricia Lewis, the daughter of Lalla Selbini and his great-niece, was the executrix of his will.

Kate Knight

Kate was born in 1863 or 1864 and her birth was registered in Southampton between January and March 1864. She was baptised at the same time as her sisters Lily and Agnes at St Luke's church in Southampton on the twelfth day of February 1865. Kate was not listed with her grandmother in the 1871

---

[13] The 1881 census lists an Agnes Knight of the same age and place of birth but it is unclear whether she is the same person as the daughter of Kate. Agnes in the census record is stated to be the sister of Archibald and Lizzie Livingston. Lizzie's maiden name was Knight but there is no Agnes listed with the Knight family in 1871. Could Lizzie's family have adopted Agnes? If so, it is a coincidence that they bear the same surname? Note also that Lizzie's family were living in Portsea in 1861, the same place that Agnes' family lived at that time. I have not found any evidence to link Lizzie's father to Agnes' father.

census although she may have been omitted in error. In 1881, she was living with the Barker sisters in Liverpool. There were three Barker sisters; Ellen Caroline, Alice Elizabeth, and Catherine Susan, the children of William and Mary Jane Barker. William was a victualler who spent some time in India where his two eldest daughters were born. The family returned to Liverpool in about 1863 which was Mary Jane's home town where their third daughter was born.

William and Mary Jane adopted Kate but precisely when they did is unknown[14]. Mary Jane died in 1874 and William died the following year so the adoption would have been before then. Kate's grandmother, Mary Chatters, had died in early 1874 and it is likely that the adoption took place soon afterwards. Kate's mother, Kate Chatters, was still performing on the stage at that time so she was possibly unable to care for her children. She had also embarked upon her affair with Henry Flowerday. It is unclear how Kate Chatters met the Barker family as she had settled in South Shields in 1874 and the Barker family was living in Liverpool. Nor is it clear why the Barkers were willing to adopt her daughter Kate. However, Kate had been very popular in Liverpool so she may have established a friendship with the Barker family on a previous occasion.

After William and Mary Jane Barker had died, Kate junior continued living with their daughters who remained spinsters. In both the 1881 and 1891 censuses, she is identified as their adopted sister. In 1881, Kate's occupation was listed as "remains at home" whereas in 1891 it is listed as "employed

---

[14] I have not found any evidence of the adoption which probably took place informally, as was usual during the nineteenth century.

at home". Perhaps she had some condition, such as agoraphobia, which prevented her from leaving the house. However, Kate obviously overcame any such problems as she married William Edward Jones, a librarian, on the twenty-sixth day of October 1891 in Everton. Ellen Caroline Barker was one of the witnesses. William and Kate did not have any children. William died at the age of eighty-four years in Liverpool on the twenty-ninth day of January 1946. Kate survived her husband by six years and she died in Broadgreen Hospital in Liverpool on the eighth day of January 1952. Her age was given as eighty-three years although she was in fact eighty-eight years old.

William John Knight

William was born in 1868 and his birth was registered in West Derby, Lancashire, between April and June. I have no information about William's whereabouts immediately after his grandmother died but he was only five or six years old so he would not have been able to fend for himself. He was almost certainly adopted, possibly by the Elton family (see below). He next reappears in the 1891 census in Bolton. He had followed his mother and eldest sister into show business and he joined up with Frank Elton.

Frank Elton was the son of William and Eliza Elton and, according to the census records he was born in Hull in about 1862 although I have not found any civil records to confirm his birth. His father William went by the name of *William Lorenzi* and he led a troupe of acrobats who performed in the music halls and circuses across Great Britain. However, there were many similar acts performing at the time and competition was fierce so Frank considered a change of

38

direction. Frank had married Rose Margaret Jordan Phillips in Oldham in 1884. Rose was the daughter of George and Jane Phillips and her father was a singer and dancer in the music halls. Rose had inherited some of his talents. So in about 1885, Frank, Rose, William [Knight] and another female, Lillian Hales[15], became the *"Sisters Phillips and Brothers Lorenzi"* who were also known as the *"Four Comical Cards"*[16] . The act performed sketches with a mixture of singing, dancing, and slapstick comedy, using original material. The first reference that I have found for the act was an advertisement by their agent, Hugh Jay Didcott, in *The Era* on the thirty-first day of October 1885:

Sisters Phillips and Brothers Lorenzi, the comical boys and curious girls, acknowledged [as] the greatest and most versatile performers extant, have made the greatest hit ever known at the Birmingham Concert Hall. [They create] a perfect furore nightly; five and six songs, gags, and curtains after curtains [encores]; on the stage one hour. Never such screams, shrieks, and applause [were] heard. And what are people saying? E. Martin says "the best act in England". Artistes say "funniest act of the day". Proprietors say "best

---

[15] Lillian was the daughter of Richard Hales, a comedian, and Jane Richards, a singer.
[16] When the act started, there was another act known as *"The Sisters and Brothers Phillips, the Three Comical Cards"* which had been formed in 1870. W. H. Phillips, their founder, ran a number of advertisements throughout 1886 claiming copyright to the name of the act and threatened legal action against any infringement. The advertisements were clearly aimed at Frank Elton's act although they did not single it out explicitly. Nevertheless, Frank's act was billed as the *"Four Comical Cards"* from early 1888 and there are no reports of any action being taken against him.

draw for months". Audience say "we never laughed so much".

Obviously, it was the agent's job to promote his artistes so, perhaps, the claims were a little exaggerated but the act was soon topping the bills at many provincial theatres. By early 1888, they had changed agents to Percy Williams and they were booked a year in advance. They toured almost continually for the next ten years, visiting many cities and major towns in England, Scotland, Ireland and continental Europe and they were the headline attraction at many of them. An article in *The Era* on the twenty-third day of July 1892 typified their schedule:

The Sisters Phillips and Brothers Lorenzi, the "four comical cards", have been making a great hit at the Eden Theatre, Ostend, in their new pantomime sketch, "The Cook's Birthday". Thence they will go to Holland, returning at the end of September to the leading London music halls. They are also engaged to play the principal parts in, and superintend the production of the pantomime of "Blue Beard" at the Shakespeare Theatre, Liverpool, at Christmas.

In 1898 and 1899, the troupe toured Australia, organised by the impresario Harry Rickards. While on tour, Frank gave an interview, which was reported on in a number of Australian newspapers:

The Phillips Sisters and the Lorenzi Brothers were all practically born in the business. The brothers began their career as acrobats and were known as the Lorenzi troupe[17].

---

[17] In 1883, the male members of the Lorenzi troupe were Harry, Fred, William, and Frank. It is unclear whether William was Frank's father or

They performed in Egypt before the Viceroy, Russia, Spain, France, Holland, Germany, and other Continental centres. '"We then found", said Mr. Lorenzi, "that the acrobatic business was going down and that the variety turns were getting into greater demand than ever, so we decided to join the ranks of the latter class. It was then that my brother and I were joined by the Sisters Phillips, and we have shown together ever since — about 9 years, if I remember rightly[18]. Our first appearance, as variety artists was at the Gaiety, Birmingham, and since then we have appeared in all the leading London and Provincial houses. Previous to leaving London we had only had a three weeks' rest during the last three years".

On their return from Australia, the troupe undertook an extensive tour of the provincial music halls and they were booked many months in advance. However, the advance bookings created a problem for them in 1900 which forced them to take legal action against the Alhambra Palace Company and others for an alleged breach of contact. They had been booked to appear at the Alhambra in Hull but before they were due to undertake the engagement, the theatre changed hands and their contract was cancelled. Since they were unable to get another engagement at short notice, they sued for loss of earnings of £55, equivalent to two weeks' fee. The judge found in their favour.

William Knight. There were also a number of female members of the troupe.

[18] His memory did not serve him rightly! The troupe had been formed in 1885, thirteen years before they undertook the tour of Australia.

The act performed regularly for the next six years and they remained firm favourites with the audiences. They appeared in pantomime; *"Babes in the Wood"* where they performed their own original songs, and *"Blue Beard: or the Barber of Bagdad's Bad Behaviour to his Beautiful Bairn"*. When out of the pantomime season, the troupe entertained audiences with two of their original sketches; *"the Cook's Birthday"* and *"the Saucy Skipper"*.

However, the act came to an abrupt end when Frank collapsed on stage while performing on stage in the "Babes in the Wood" pantomime at a theatre in Eccles. He died of heart failure two days later at his home in Eccles on the nineteenth day of February 1906 at the age of forty-two years. His death was reported in the *Bolton Evening News* on the twentieth day of February 1906:

The death occurred at Eccles on Monday of a well-known Bolton comedian, in the person of Francis Elton, at the age of 44 years (sic). Deceased was in partnership with his brother and travelled under the name of Brothers Lorenzi, the Sisters Philips being associated with them. These artists had frequently appeared at the Grand while they have also appeared with Mr. J F Elliston's pantomime.

Ironically, a week later one newspaper reported that the producer of "Babes in the Wood" was planning to take the show to Aberdeen with the Sisters Phillips and Brothers Lorenzi as the star attractions. A review of the pantomime in the *Dundee Courier* dated the sixth day of March incorrectly stated:

Mr Frank Lorenzi and Mr William Lorenzi, as the two ruffians, proved themselves excellent comedians of the knockabout species.

Perhaps the paper had taken their names from the programme although Frank could not have appeared in the actual show. It is possible that William fulfilled the engagement with a stand-in for Frank.

There is strong evidence supporting the date that Frank died. Apart from his death announcement, his family continued placing "in memoriam" notices for a number of subsequent years confirming the date.

Frank had been the driving force behind the act and, after his death, the troupe disbanded. Frank's wife, Rose Phillips, continued to live in their family home in Bolton which she ran as a boarding house for show business people. I have no further information on Lillie.

William Knight continued in show business under the name of William Lorenzi. He appeared in comic roles in pantomimes for a number of years such as:

- "Dick Whittington" in Hull in early 1908
- "Babes in the Wood" at the Elephant and Castle in early 1909 where he played "Nurse Wilhemina Wilkins"
- "Dick Whittington" in Sheffield in early 1910 where he played "Captain Tarpaulin"
- "The Forty Thieves" in Salford in 1913/14

William also appeared in musical comedies; "Schnapps of Rotterdam" in Eastbourne in July 1912, and in the revue "Spots" which toured the country and ran from about August 1915 through to January 1917. He then formed a comedy partnership with Mr Hart (first name not known) and they appeared as the *Lorenzi Brothers* in provisional theatres throughout the 1920s. The partnership was dissolved in 1928.

The last record that I have found relating to William's stage career is when he appeared in 1930 in an American comedy called "the Meddler" in Leeds. He played the part of "Mr Parker, a customer".

William married Bertha Bailey in Croydon on the twenty-fourth day of July 1927. He was 59 years old and Bertha was 47 years old. Bertha was born in Croydon on the seventeenth day of November 1879, the daughter of James Bailey, a groom, and his wife Jane. Although Bertha did not come from a show business family, she took the stage name Maudie Bignell and performed as a singer. There is very little information in the papers regarding her performances which suggests that she was not very successful. Indeed, the 1939 register lists her occupation as "Wardrobe Mistress Theatre (retired)" rather than "variety artist". William and Bertha met before 1912. They placed a joint advertisement in *The Stage* in March 1912 declaring their availability for work[19]. I do not have any evidence that William and Bertha performed together.

William died in 1934 at his home in Lambeth of acute bronchitis. His death was reported in *The Stage* on the eleventh day of January 1934:

LORENZI – Passed peacefully away January 4, 1934, William John Knight Lorenzi, late of the Sisters Phillips and

---

[19] It was common at the time for artistes to advertise their availability for work through the wants adverts in the trade magazines.

Brothers Lorenzi, beloved husband of Maudie Bignell. Rest in peace.

The Stage also reported on the fourteenth day of January 1937:

Friends of Mrs Maude Bignell (Lorenzi) will be sorry to hear that she is lying seriously ill in Dulwich Hospital, H2 Ward, where she will be pleased to hear from friends.

Maude (Bertha) survived her illness and she died in 1945 at the age of sixty-five years. Her death was registered at Lewes in Sussex between January andMarch.

Note: There was an article published in the Dundee Evening Telegraph dated the ninth day of June 1932 by David Keir Gracie, A dancer and actor, who recounts his meeting William and Maude when he was on the same bill in about 1912. Some of his information is in conflict with my research and I suspect that he had confused the career of the early Lorenzis with the career of William and Maude.

Part 2:

The Great
Selbinis

French publicity poster for the Selbinis, 1889
(Source: https://www.flickr.com/photos/bibliodyssey/15641407766)

Jack Selbini

Jack in 1894(Source: The Sketch, October 17, 1894)

Kate's daughter, Lily, also had a life in show business and she was part of the world famous Selbini Troupe. Her husband was John Selbini, known as Jack, who was born Patrick Joseph McCoy in Westfield, Massachusetts in America in 1855, the son of Irish immigrant parents, Patrick and Catherine McCoy.

Records for Jack's parents, Patrick and Catherine, are incomplete so it is difficult to establish their definitive history. According to the 1861 UK census, they had a daughter, Mary, who was born in Hanley in the county of Staffordshire (now part of Stoke-on-Trent) in about 1852, although I have failed to find a record for her in the civil birth register. There are no entries for the family in the Massachusetts immigration records, nor are they listed in the 1855 census for the state. Neither is there a birth or baptism record for Jack; the evidence that he was born in Westfield in 1855 is from a newspaper report of an interview that he gave when he was an adult. It appears that Patrick and Catherine first moved to Hanley to escape the potato famine in Ireland and then they immigrated to America. It is possible that they travelled to

Canada from England as the fare was considerably cheaper than travelling directly to America. They would have then crossed the border into New England where many Irish immigrants settled and it may explain why there are no immigration records of the family entering Massachusetts[20].

Patrick was an unskilled labourer and although work was probably plentiful, living conditions in Massachusetts were extremely harsh. A health committee report on Boston in 1849 following an outbreak of cholera illustrated the poor living conditions[21]:

"The average age of Irish life in Boston does not exceed fourteen years. In Broad Street and all the entire surrounding neighbourhood, including Fort Hill and the adjacent streets, the situation of the Irish is particularly wretched. During their visits last summer, your committee were witnesses of scenes too painful to be forgotten, and yet too disgusting to be related here. It is sufficient to say, that the whole district is a perfect hive of human beings, without comforts and mostly without common necessaries; in many cases, huddled together like brutes, without regard to sex, or age, or sense of decency: grown men and women sleeping together in the same apartment, and sometimes wife and husband, brothers and sisters all in the same bed."

---

[20] The British Passenger Acts attempted to deflect the emigration from the British Isles to Canada instead of the U.S., making the fare a cheap 15 shillings compared to the 4 or 5 pounds sterling fare to New York. Many Irish soon found it convenient to take the affordable trip to Canada, where they could buy cheap fares to the U.S., or cheaper yet, they could walk across the border.
[21] Reproduced courtesy of *Spartacus Educational*.

Probably disillusioned by life in Massachusetts, the family moved back to England before 1861 and returned to Hanley where Jack spent his early childhood. Patrick senior, Catherine, and Mary are listed in the 1871 census living at 15, Swan Street in Hanley. Patrick was working as a furnace man in an iron foundry. Many families of Irish descent were living in Swan Street at that time. Patrick died in 1882 and his death was registered in Stoke-on-Trent between October and December. I have not found the family in the 1881 census; nor have I found a death record for Catherine. Of course, Catherine may have remarried although I have not found any evidence.

Jack started travelling with the Powell and Clark's circus from Londonderry in about 1864 from the age of nine years where, as an apprentice, he learned horse-riding, leaping, and nearly every trick connected with a travelling circus. However, he was not happy and, as soon as the opportunity arose, he ran away. He joined up with a small travelling show[22] and he then became a pupil of George Gorin, later known as George Letine[23]. Gorin formed a bicycle troupe with Jack, a girl

---

[22] At the time of the 1871 census, the show was touring in Monmouthshire and Jack is listed as John McCoy, living in a caravan with travellers Joseph and Elizabeth Baker. He is also described as a traveller and his occupation as a servant. The proprietor of the show was Ellen Stevens, a thirty-five year old widow.

[23] George Letine was murdered in 1889 by Nathaniel Curragh, who stabbed him when he left the Canterbury Theatre in London after a performance. Curragh's daughter had been part of Letine's troupe but she left it after a year, suffering from consumption (tuberculosis) from which she subsequently died. Curragh accused Letine and his wife of ill-treating his daughter although, after many fruitless court cases in which nothing was proven, Curragh finally snapped and killed Letine. He then shot himself in the mouth but he did not die and he was tried for the murder. He was

known as Mademoiselle Rosina, and another man, William Villion[24] and they obtained engagements in Germany, Austria, and Hungary. Jack was originally used as an acrobat and contortionist and he was known as "the caoutchouc man" [rubber man]. He developed his bicycle act in Vienna in 1875 on an old "bone shaker," with iron tyres and wooden wheels. He had to roughen the tyres with a chisel to prevent them from slipping on the stage. Jack used to perform such tricks as riding about among lighted bottles, and eating his supper and drinking a bottle of beer off a tray on the handle-bars while riding round the stage.

In a newspaper article in 1916, it stated that Jack was "practically the originator of trick cycling, his only rival being Professor Brown[25], who was also known by the less dignified appellation of *Old Jock Brown*." Professor Brown was almost certainly Henry Brown who began trick cycling in 1869, six years before Jack, but he failed to achieve the same success.

Gorin's troupe was originally called *Young Brown's Troupe*, perhaps as an acknowledgement to Henry Brown's pioneering work, but Gorin soon changed the name of the troupe to *Gorin's Velocipede Company*. The troupe met with splendid receptions in Europe and it seems that Jack was the star of the act judging from the newspaper reports at that time. Jack later claimed that he was one of the instigators in setting up the

---

acquitted on the grounds of insanity.
[24] William's real name was William Stephen Bexfield and he was born in London in 1853, the son of Stephen Bexfield and Harriett Cooper Andrews.
[25] According to the *Guinness Book of Records*, trick cycling was introduced by Ancillotti in Italy in 1868. Perhaps the first act to appear in Britain were three young boys from Glasgow, who, at the end of 1868, formed a short-lived trick cycling act known as the *Three Petit Lavalles*.

troupe. He was certainly an innovator in developing the act and he was a big risk taker, performing very dangerous feats. He may indeed have been the main driver but it is more likely that Gorin, as the more experienced man in the circus business, took the lead and provided the finances. However, the troupe was short-lived and Jack teamed up with William Villion in early 1876.

The Villion and Selbini Troupe

Known originally as "Villion and Selbini", the following newspaper advertisement described their performance:

Velocipedian Wonders, VILLION and SELBINI, the only somersault acts on velocipedes in Europe and the greatest American contortionist, the Man Frog and Man Serpent. The only artists that throw backward and forward somersaults on velocipedes, we have been engaged to give twenty special performances at the GRAND THIER GARDENS, [BUDA]PEST, HUNGARY. We are not killed yet and will shortly arrive in England.

No doubt, the last comment was tongue in cheek! On their return to England in late 1876, Jack and William undertook an eight-week engagement at the Theatre Royal in Covent Garden where they appeared before the Prince and Princess of Wales [later King Edward VII and Queen Alexandria]. It was during this performance that Jack met with his only serious accident. In his own words:

"I did my flip-flap back trick, and overturned, with the result that, instead of my feet reaching the ground at an angle, the toes came together, and my ankle snapped like a carrot. The snap could be heard all over the house. I did not, in my excitement, however, notice what had happened, and I jumped up and finished the performance with my partner. But when I got to the wings, I found that the fractured bones of my foot were protruding, and I fainted. The next thing I remember was being in Charing Cross Hospital".

The act was very successful and appeared across the country throughout 1877 in such places as Bradford, Nottingham,

Lowestoft, the Isle of Man, and Gloucester. At the end of the year, Jack and William returned to Germany and it was there that Jack met Lily Knight. Lily had just started out on her own stage career as a characteristic vocalist and dancer, following in the footsteps of her mother, Kate Chatters. She had appeared at the London Theatre in Sheffield in July 1876 and at the Corn Exchange in Derby in August 1876 but I have not found evidence of any other engagements in England. It may be that she was working in Germany when she met Jack or she may simply have been on holiday. She and Jack married in 1878 and the marriage was registered in Southampton between April and June.

Jack and Lily had five children:

- Mary Elizabeth, known as Lalla, was born in Douglas on the Isle of Man on the twenty-eighth day of August 1878.
- Charles Alexander was born in Glasgow on the twenty-sixth day of February 1880 and he died on his first birthday on the twenty-sixth day of February 1881. His death was registered in Marylebone.
- Victor, was born in Scotland in about 1881[26].
- Leola Lily was born in Lowestoft in the county of Suffolk on the thirteenth day of August 1882.

---

[26] The date and place of birth are derived from the 1891 census. Jack and Lily were in America at the supposed time of Victor's birth. It is possible that he was adopted. In an interview in 1895, Jack stated that his troupe consisted of himself, his wife, his three daughters, his son, and two young men. The reference to a son is almost certainly referring to Victor. It is unlikely that Victor was born in 1880 if he was the natural son of Jack and Lily. Their first son (Charles) was born in February of that year and Lily was active on the stage in November and December (probably the earliest date when Victor would have been born).

- Mizpah Agnes was born in Aston in the county of Warwickshire on the fifteenth day of February 1886.

Jack and William's act went from strength to strength. A review of their performance at the Victoria Rink in Southampton in April 1878 in the *Mid-Weekly Hampshire* newspaper describes their act and the reception that they received:

One of the most attractive performances among the many for which the Victoria has from time to time been celebrated, is the engagement of Messrs Villion and Selbini, two extraordinary velocipede acrobats, whose feats are novel, astonishing and numerous. They embrace some daring riding, done either jointly or separately, with dexterity perfectly astonishing, the more so as some clever juggling is executed meanwhile; such a storm of applause was never before heard at the rink that met Selbini's imitation by means of swirling torches of a fiery Catherine wheel while mounted on the shoulders of his co-performer who is spinning around at a terrific rate, and finishing by bringing the bicycle to a standstill; to reach the ground the mounter concludes with turning a somersault. These artists have drawn together very large and fashionable audiences every night, the attraction being, no doubt, on account of them varying their programme each evening.

Lily joined the act soon after her first child, Lalla, was born, and a second female, William's wife Lizzie, joined a few months after that, presumably to add glamour and some more variety. The act was now known as the *Villion and Selbini* (later, the *Selbini and Villion) Troupe*.

(Source: Der Deutsche correspondent. (Baltimore, Md.), 02 April 1881.
Chronicling America: Historic American Newspapers)

For the next three years, they appeared throughout the United Kingdom and Europe in places such as Great Yarmouth, Aberdeen, Glasgow, Dublin, Wolverhampton, Liverpool, Chester, Hull, London, Spain, and France, many of the engagements being with Hengler's Circus. Various other artistes were added to the act from time to time, perhaps to stand in for the females when they took maternity breaks. For example, an ex-member of the troupe placed an advertisement in the *Era* (trade newspaper) in November 1879:

Notice to Bicycle Troupes; ALPHA (pupil to Selbini) is prepared to make an engagement as a trick bicycle rider, mounter, back and forward somersaults off the shoulders, and posturing. A troupe of acrobats may write.

In 1880, the troupe appeared at the Cirque D'Ete and the Folies Bergère in Paris, and at the Circi De Price in Madrid before the King and Queen of Spain.

The highlight of the troupe's career was their engagement on a lengthy tour of America with Forepaugh's Circus and they set sail on the tenth day of March 1881 on the *SS Helvetia*. Jack and Lily's daughter Lalla stayed behind in England at the home of an elderly farmer, James Cooper, and his wife at Lowestoft in the county of Suffolk.

The act appeared to be successful in America. They received positive reviews and their appearance at Fort Dodge in Iowa was described as follows:

The first appearance here of the Old World's latest sensation THE GREAT SELBINI & VILLION TROUPE of gymnastic bicyclers. They turn somersaults from shoulder to shoulder, stand erect upon each other's heads, three [members of the troupe] resting on the wheelman. Two, three and four [members of the troupe] form pyramids and engage in juggling and all manner of surprising feats, all done up on bicycles dashing around at a twenty mile speed.

When Jack was travelling on the circus train in Missouri, it met with a disastrous collision where many persons and animals perished. The Selbini and Villion Troupe only escaped through being expert gymnasts and taking pantomime leaps through the windows as the carriage rolled over, thus leaving them free to help to save others who were less fortunate.

I have failed to find a newspaper report of the incident although it appears that the trains carrying circus animals and personnel crashed on many occasions. There is a report of a train crashing in West Virginia when a carriage containing the elephants rolled down an embankment and two men were killed, although the date of the incident is not known. A crash in Philadelphia in 1885 was reported in the *New York Times* which claimed it was the sixth time that Forepaugh's train had crashed in the current season.

Such incidents were common for all circus owners in the late nineteenth century, often with fatalities to animals and people.

Separation

The partnership between Jack and William was dissolved in about August 1881 in St Louis while they were on tour in America. Whether the split was amicable or not is debatable and the reason for it is unclear. It may be that they both felt that the act had been taken as far as it could and no doubt there were now a number of similar acts around the world. Jack teamed up with Lily and William teamed up with his wife and each act continued to perform in America. Jack put the following advertisement in the *New York Clipper* in September:

M Selbini and Mlle Lily, the greatest European Bicycle equestrians, Jugglers and Equilibrists on bicycles who have ever visited America. The world's champion bicyclists. We challenge the universe to produce our equals. Now performing with great success with Forepaugh's Great Circus. Notice to proprietors and managers. Having dissolved partnership with W Villion, for the future we will be known as **M Selbini and Mlle Selbini, the champion bicyclists.** *Can arrange with managers of first class halls, "Humpty Dumpty" Co. and travelling troupes for the coming winter season. Address care of Clipper.*

Meanwhile, William formed his own rival troupe by replacing Jack with another acrobat and he placed his own advertisement in the *New York Clipper* in October:

VILLION TROUPE, bicycle equestrians, (one lady and two gentlemen), jugglers, somersault acts, pyramids, etc on bicycles. NB – to managers and directors – Having left Selbini, I have secured the services of an American Bicycle

Artist, Juggler, and Somersault Act Rider, which makes my troupe the greatest now travelling in America, and acknowledged by the press and public to be the biggest novelty now with Forepaugh's Great Aggregation and Circus. Just concluded six month's engagement, and re-engaged until December to go South. Address: Clipper Office, New York, USA. Kind regards to friends.

The Villion troupe continued to perform in America for the next three years and they then took up engagements in Europe.

The Selbinis completed a further six months in America with Forepaugh's circus and then they returned to England. Lily was heavily pregnant with their second daughter at that time so they would not have been able to undertake any further engagements. The following article, presumably placed by Jack himself to gain publicity, appeared in the press in July 1882 on their return:

Just arrived from America, the European Magnets and World's Champion Bicyclist, J Selbini and Mme Lily, after a most highly successful and brilliant tour of fifteen months throughout America. We were the sensation with M.B. Leavitt's All Star Speciality Combination in San Francisco, California, and we were acknowledged by press, public, and managers of America to have no equals in our line of business. A few opinions of the California press: San Francisco News Letter, January 14th 1882 "Speaking of the best first, the bicycle performance of J Selbini and Mdlle Lily is entitled to the primary word of praise. It is more wonderful than any bicycle performance ever seen here, and the balancing is simply marvellous. Imagine Miss Lily standing on the shoulders of Selbini tearing around the stage on a bicycle without any handle to guide it, tossing balls, knives, and lighted torches, and you get an idea of the perfection of balancing and the capabilities of a bicycle." Daily Examiner, San Francisco, January 29th 1882 "The bicycle act of Selbini and his pretty and graceful little wife is the wonder of the spectators." J Selbini and Mdlle Lilly are now taking a few weeks' recreation previous to their commencing engagements again.

The move back to England was the start of Jack's plan to establish a family troupe.

The Selbinis – Evolving the Act

On their return from America in 1882, Lily gave birth to their second daughter, Leola Lily, in Lowestoft. Jack and Lily then recommenced touring and they recruited another female acrobat to work with them.[27] They introduced their young daughter, Lalla, who had just had her fourth birthday, into the act to perform simple tricks on a bicycle. They billed themselves as:

The European Magnets and World's Champion Bicyclists, the Selbini Troupe (four in number), world-renowned and incomparable male and female bicyclists. J Selbini, the Marvel, and Mlle Lily, the most graceful lady bicyclist in the world, Mlle Jeannette the Accomplished, and Baby Lalla, smallest and cleverest baby bicyclist in the universe. The whole forming one of the grandest bicycle displays ever witnessed.

The troupe embarked upon a provincial tour of the United Kingdom appearing in Glasgow, Hull, Swansea, Bristol, Cardiff, Dublin and London (and possibly other venues) over the next ten months. It is possible that Jack and Lily adopted their son Victor (assuming that they had adopted him) when they visited Glasgow.

When appearing at the Metropolitan Music Hall in the Edgware Road in London on the twenty-first day of October 1882, and while they were on stage, an employee of the theatre, Edward Buck, allegedly entered their dressing room

---

[27] Billed as Mlle Jeanette, the Accomplished, her inclusion in the act was short-lived and the troupe had reverted to a trio by January of the following year.

and stole a purse containing two diamond rings and eighteen shillings in money. The stolen items were never found. Buck was acquitted of the charge of larceny.

During the tour, the inclusion of Lalla into the act proved a huge success and the troupe were booked to tour America again. They set sail from Liverpool on the eighteenth day of August 1883 to undertake a two-year American tour with Michael B. Leavitt's company. Leavitt was an American entrepreneur who set up tours to rural areas, importing the best acts from Europe so it was quite an accolade for the Selbinis to be included in his show. Leavitt claimed to have been the first person to use the term *vaudeville* to describe his variety shows.

Although the show contained thirty-six different acts, the Selbinis received excellent reviews and, when in California, they were singled out as a special attraction:

The Selbini Family accomplish many skilful and daring feats upon the bicycle, to which is added the execution of similar tricks by Baby Selbini, much to the entertainment of adults and amusement of the youngsters.

However, their success resulted in Jack being arrested for child cruelty! *The Daily Alta* (Californian daily newspaper) reported on the first day of April 1884:

A Specialist in Trouble

M Selbini, the head of the Selbini family, one of the chief attractions of Leavitt's European Specialty Company, was arrested at the Brooklyn Hotel yesterday by Officer Holbrook and charged with cruelty to children. Last Sunday, the accused exhibited "Baby" Selbini, aged three years, before a *large audience at Woodward's Gardens. At first, she simply rode a small bicycle for four minutes. This performance the authorities had agreed to allow, but when the tot was encored, she appeared on the stage in company with the accused, and went through several difficult and exhaustive acrobatic feats, which caused his arrest. Selbini went before Judge Yost after his arrest and upon pleading that there was no intent on his part to violate the law he was allowed to put up $20 bail instead of the normal $50.*

"Baby" (Lalla) was five and a half years old at the time and she was probably quite capable of performing her act without being forced to do so by her parents. Perhaps they believed that it was more appealing to the audience if they pretended that Lalla was younger than her actual age but, as far as Californian law went, that was a mistake. In the circumstances, the show moved on to Utah the following day and no further action was taken, the bail money being forfeited.

The Selbinis continued to be star attractions and the audiences in Salt Lake City were equally as enthusiastic as those in California. Following an appearance at the Salt Lake Theatre on the fourth day of April 1884, the local paper reported:

The audience were delighted to the verge of enthusiasm by the wonderful bicycling feats of the Selbini family, father, mother, and child, who performed on their bicycles something after the fashion of the champion circus riders on horseback. The child, a mere baby, dressed in a cunning little costume consisting of two silk flags, took the house by storm, fascinating some members of the audience to such an extent that they threw silver quarters and half dollars to her on the stage.

The American tour continued for another year and the Selbinis recruited a fourth member, J Alpha[28]. When appearing in Tennessee and Kentucky in August 1884, they were described as *"French bicycle riders, the best and acknowledged champions of the world"*!

They continued to win over the American audiences as, for example, the favourable review that they received when they performed in Providence in the state of Maryland in March 1885:

The Selbini troupe carried off the honours of the evening in the athletic line performing on bicycles such astonishing feats of agility and complicated evolutions as no man would believe possible until he witnessed them. The troupe consists of J Selbini, Mlle Lily, Baby Lalla, and J Alpha, who would in themselves be welcomed warmly for their fine stage business. Their act is at all time difficult, and is free from any suggestive position, and is polished by the cute actions of the little child. This little one will be a great favourite with children of Providence families.

On their return to England in June 1885, the Selbinis joined Hengler's Grand Cirque [circus], appearing in Dublin for about six weeks before touring the north of England visiting Scarborough, Hull, and other places. They then appeared with

---

[28] In 1879, when Jack was performing with William Villion, a person called Alpha, who had been a pupil of Jack's, advertised for a position as a trick bicycler and acrobat. He is possibly the same person who later joined the Selbinis on their American tour.

Ohmy's circus before returning to Hengler's circus for a further ten months when they appeared in London, Hanley (where Jack was raised as a child), and Blackpool. By October of that year, Jack and Lily had added their second daughter, Leola, to the act at the tender age of three years. The act was now receiving star billing, as reported in the *Hull Packet* on the second day of October:

Mr Hengler comes before us with stronger claims for support than ever. The great attraction this time is undoubtedly the Selbini family, in their truly marvellous family entertainment. The family consists of two gentlemen [Jack and Alpha], a lady [Lily], and two children [Lalla and Leola], and each of them goes through some astonishing tricks – tricks which it is almost impossible to believe are capable of being done unless seen. A large circular wooden "track" is put down and over this in mazy circles glide these clever bicyclists. Riding with one leg with the other leg over the handle is child's play to them; they ride with one leg, while the other is twisted round their neck, with the greatest ease; and they think nothing of going round the little circle at full speed juggling with four balls, or spinning half a dozen plates at once. It is surprising to see them standing on each others' shoulders, riding without handles, or standing on their heads in the saddle, but the applause, always loud, assumes deafening proportions when one of the male riders takes the backbone and back wheel off his bicycle, and travels rapidly round the ring on one wheel[29]. It would not be possible, in a short newspaper notice, to mention all the tricks these exceedingly, we may truly say wonderfully, clever family perform. It is difficult to believe –

---

[29] Lalla later, as an adult, developed this act for herself.

unless seen, of course – that any person could have the control over such a wayward thing as a bicycle as these Selbinis have, and those who have seen them will indeed wonder at the apparent ease with which they go through their seemingly impossible, and at times sensational, tricks. This part of the programme is in itself worth a visit, and none of our readers should miss seeing the Selbinis.

The Selbinis left Hengler's circus at the end of 1885, to be replaced by the Villion Troupe, the act set up by Jack's former partner, William Villion.

After the Villion Troupe had completed their tour of America, they carried out a number of engagements in Continental Europe, visiting Berlin, Hanover, Breslau, Kola, Leopzig, St Petersburg, Moscow, Kiev, Warsaw, Liege, and Antwerp. They returned to England at the end of 1885 and they teamed up with Joe Mendoza[30]. They described themselves as "champion tumblers of Europe and America, acrobatic bicyclists and monocyclists". The act included "little May Villion, l'incomparable", William's daughter who was born in America in about 1882. It is likely that the Villions saw (or heard about) the Selbini act when it went to America and they were inspired by its success to establish a similar act for themselves. The troupe had a number of engagements in England throughout 1886 and, as part of Hengler's circus, they appeared before Queen Victoria at Windsor Castle on the twenty-fifth day of February 1886 but they left the circus soon afterwards. Another act featuring infant cyclists appeared

---

[30] Joe may have been part of the Villion troupe when they performed in Europe. I cannot find any references to him as a solo act before he teamed up with the Villions.

about the same time. "Lotto's one-wheeled wonders" included infant bicyclists Lotto, Lilo, and Otto and they were appearing at the Royal Princess's Theatre, Glasgow.

Meanwhile, the Selbini Troupe was performing at the Grand Theatre in Birmingham and they continued to get excellent reviews. The *Birmingham Daily Mail* reported:

Another remarkable subject of interest is the phenomenal bicycling of the Selbini troupe. A detailed description of their marvellous feats has already appeared in our columns, but it would be a great injustice to Mr Melville's enterprise not to repeat the admiration we have previously expressed for the daring and elegant skills of the Selbinis. What the two tiny children of the troupe do is scarcely credible even when witnessed, for it seems impossible that things so small can have such a control over their bicycles. This performance was received with enthusiasm on Saturday night, and is certain to be one of the strongest attractions of the Grand.

The daughters, Lalla and Leola, were presented with medals by the proprietor of the Grand. However, Lily was not performing with the troupe at this time. She gave birth to her third daughter, Mizpah, on the fifteenth day of February 1886. The act was now firmly established as a star attraction and, following Lily's confinement, it was in great demand.

They received invitations to perform from both America and Europe but Jack initially turned down such offers, probably because Lily was pregnant with their third daughter, Mizpah. However, they accepted an offer of a ten-month tour in America from July 1887 with the Slavin and Johnson Minstrel Company, leaving Mizpah in England.

The tour gave the troupe the opportunity to establish themselves as a world-class act and they received glowing reports. The *Rome [Georgia] Daily Sentinel* wrote on the twenty-sixth day of January 1888:

The Selbini family, bicyclists, plate spinners and tumblers, gave a marvellous exhibition. Mr and Mrs Selbini and their three children[31] are wonderfully good performers in their line. The children are probably the most expert juvenile bicycle riders in the world. Their performance brought out thunders of applause and an encore.

At the end of the ten month tour of America with Slavin and Johnson, Lily had a solo career for a brief time. Perhaps she and Jack had a falling-out and they decided upon a trial separation? I cannot think of another obvious reason as to why Lily would leave her husband and children. If she had simply wanted to go solo, she could have achieved that ambition while staying with her family.

Jack and the children returned to England but Lily remained in America. She had her own solo juggling act and she placed an advertisement in the *New York Clipper* on the second day of June 1888:

---

[31] The three children were Lalla, Victor and an apprentice, William. Leola was ill and she did not tour with them when they went to America (see later).

Meanwhile, Jack and the rest of the troupe performed for a short while in England. On the same day that Lily placed her advertisement in the *New York Clipper*, Jack placed an advertisement in *The Era* (the trade paper for the music halls) which was published in London:

The troupe undertook an engagement at the Star Music Hall in Liverpool for about six weeks and, again, they met with an enthusiastic reception from the audiences:

The leading new sensation of the week at the "Star" was the extraordinary performances of the Selbini troupe, described as the world's champion trick bicyclists, jugglers, and hat spinners. The enthusiasm aroused by the marvellous feats of these artists was something extraordinary, culminating when a very diminutive lady named Lalla most coolly and cleverly executed several wonderful feats on a bicycle.

Jack and the children returned to America in August 1888, having secured a further ten months' contract with the Slavin and Johnson Minstrels. Fred Etoile, an acrobat, joined the troupe for the tour.

Meanwhile, Lily secured work as a solo artiste and she joined Harry Kernell's New Company. Harry started in show business in an Irish Comedy Singing Act with his brother but he later turned to producing his own show. Lily remained with the company for about ten months, which appeared at a number of theatres across the country from New York to California. Lily's act received brief, but favourable reviews:

The globe running by Lillie Selbini was very good, and acquired interest from the trained birds she introduced during her performance.

Jack and the children went from strength to strength appearing across America in places such as Indianapolis, Kansas City, Duluth [Minneapolis], and Buffalo. However, their act had to be modified from time to time when concern was expressed on the possible dangers to the children. In Philadelphia, the children were prevented from taking part in the acrobatic elements although they were able to perform their cycling turns. The restrictions in New York were more severe and the children were not allowed to perform at all. The *New York Mirror* reported in December 1888:

The Selbini Family, cyclists, were to appear but owing to the advanced ideas of Mr Gerry[32] on the subject, the children were restrained. Prof Selbini appeared alone and did some marvellous riding.

The setback in New York did not deter the troupe from appearing further at other venues and they continued to be singled out in the press reports as special attractions "not to be missed". Lalla's status within the troupe continued to rise and she was fast becoming a star attraction along with her father.

Jack and the children returned to England in May 1889 but Lily remained in America with Kernell's Company until June of that year even though it seems that she was ready to return to her family. Presumably, she was under contract and she was obliged to fulfil it.

---

[32] Elbridge T Gerry was the founder of the New York Society for the Prevention of Cruelty to Children. I assume that the objection was the belief that the children's lives were endangered by performing on the stage. NY also had laws regarding child entertainers which the NYSPCC had the responsibility for enforcing so it may have been that the act was in breach of one of these laws.

The Selbinis –World Class Performers

On his return to England, Jack placed an advertisement in the press on the eighteenth day of May 1889:

THE MARVELLOUS SELBINIS and MISS LALLA, the wonder of the 19ᵗʰ century. Just arrived from America after two years successful engagement with Johnson and Slavin's greatest Minstrel Show on earth, where we were the talk of America. Thanking all American proprietors for their kind offers, as we intend to make a tour of Europe, opening at the Folies Bergère, Paris, May 25ᵗʰ. All communications addressed to the World's Champion Acrobatic Bicyclists, Jugglers, Posturers, Equilibrists, Unicyclists, etc, Oak Tree Cottage, New Wanstead, Essex, London.

On her return from America, Lily finally rejoined her family and the act. Whatever had been the cause of their separation, the problem had been resolved. The troupe expanded to six members and they made appearances in Norwich, Rochdale, Brighton and London. They rejoined Hengler's Grand Cirque[33] after a four-year break, this time as star performers, and they opened at the Drill Hall in Bristol on the twenty-ninth day of August 1889 for four weeks. They were celebrating ten years with Hengler although, of course, the act first appeared as the Selbini and Villion Troupe (in Dublin on the fourth day of June 1879). The Selbinis were now firmly established as a star attraction and audiences continued to be amazed by their act.

---

[33] The circus was founded by Charles Hengler who was proprietor when the Selbinis first appeared with them. Charles had died in 1887 and his son, Albert Hengler, was proprietor when the Selbinis rejoined the circus.

The Liverpool Daily Post reported on the eighteenth day of November 1889:

The Selbini troupe of bicyclists was also a source of great attraction. They were again and again greeted with rounds of applause for their manifold acts, which rise to a climax of difficulty and daring which one could hardly realise without seeing it. Let those who imagine that they have looked at all that is to be seen in bicycling suspend their judgment until they have seen the Selbinis, who seemed to have reached the top of the tree, not only in bicycling but in acrobatics generally.

After nine months of touring with Hengler's Grand Cirque, the troupe undertook another tour of Europe and they appeared at the Ronacher Concert Hall in Vienna where they received great acclaim:

Since the commencement of this establishment, there has been no speciality number which met with such a success as the Selbini Troupe, who are at present performing with their daring and elegant acrobatic performance on the bicycle. The public are taken by storm, and applaud enthusiastically. More extraordinary are a boy and a little girl of this company, the first as a clown who exhibits a wonderful quickness on one wheel; his little sister performs the most difficult tricks à la Kaufmann, with a playful eagerness. The public must really see for themselves the performance of this wonderful family to believe that in this line of business so many new tricks can be so wonderfully executed.

With the invention of the safety bicycle (supposedly by an Englishman, Harry John Lawson in 1876) and its rapid development, cycling became very popular and specialist magazines appeared for the enthusiasts. As the Selbinis were pioneers in the use of bicycles, it is not surprising that they had an influence on the growing pastime. The following light-hearted article in the *Cycling and Cyclists* section in the *Pall Mall Gazette* on the twenty-sixth day of December 1890 makes interesting reading:

*I saw the Selbini troupe at the Alhambra for the first time the other evening and thought their performance was clever and graceful. What a pity the pretty black and white costume of the woman rider can't give a tip to the many correspondents who keep asking "Violet Lorne" of **Bicycling News** what they ought to wear on their machines. To see her spinning lightly on her bicycle is enough to fill with envy all the poor women whose skirts make even the mounting of a tricycle a trouble.*

The act was by now almost continuously performing both in Great Britain and in Continental Europe. Their itinerary for 1891 to 1893 illustrates just how busy they were. Places where they performed include London, Paris, Copenhagen, Christiana [Denmark], Dresden, Elberfeld [Germany], Berlin, South Shields, Sunderland, Hartlepool, Newcastle, Edinburgh, Glasgow, Oxford, Canterbury, Birmingham, Manchester, Shrewsbury, Belfast, Cardiff, Brighton, and Chatham. The troupe made many repeat performances at a number of the venues. By about 1894, the troupe was continuously booked three years in advance.

The Selbini Troupe in 1894[34]:
(back row), William, Fred Etoile, Jack, Lily; (front row) Leola, Victor,
Lalla
(Source: The Sketch, October 17, 1894)

The troupe was considered by many to be the best in the world, not least by Jack himself who threw down a challenge to his contemporaries, in the sum of £500, that they could not perform the feats his troupe performed on the stage. It is not clear whether there were any takers!

What had started as a three-person act (Jack, Lily, and Lalla) eventually became an eight-person act. Jack gradually introduced his other daughters Leola and Mizpah into the troupe from an early age. Victor was introduced into the act in about 1887, at the age of about six years, providing a touch of

---

[34] Why was Mizpah missing from the photograph? She was eight years old when the photograph was taken and she had probably started to perform with the family act.

comedy. He is listed as Jack's son in the 1891 census and according to the census, he was born in Scotland but I have not been able to establish when he was adopted by Jack and Lily. The troupe appeared in Glasgow in 1883 so that may have been the time when they met Victor.

Jack extended their act to include combinations of trick-cycling, acrobatics, juggling, comedy, and music. It was probably this combination of different skills that made them unique and why they were considered the best amongst their contemporaries. In an article by William Archer in the *Contemporary Review* in March 1895, he dismissed the artistic value of music-halls as "pseudo-aesthetic cant" but he accepted that the London music halls had the best acrobats and jugglers in the world because they paid the highest wages. He cited the Selbini cycling troupe as part of this elite group.

Jack Selbini set up his base in London in Chancery Lane where he had a private gymnasium built. The gymnasium was twenty-four feet square and Jack believed that, if his troupe could perform their cycling routines and acrobatics in the gymnasium, they could perform their act on any stage. He fitted the gymnasium with an apparatus called a lunge. It was a belt attached to a rope which passed through a pulley in the ceiling. The belt was placed around the novice's waist and a rope was held at the other end. If, in attempting any trick, the learner lost his balance, the rope was pulled tight to prevent him (or her) from falling. The training would take place for about twelve months before the novice was considered able to maintain his (or her) balance without any aids.

Jack established a rigorous schedule for all the members of the troupe requiring three hours training for their cycling and acrobatic feats and a further couple of hours in the afternoon training on their musical performance before performing their act in the evening. He also ensured that they had a regulated diet with plenty of meat to ensure that they had sufficient strength and stamina to perform. And, in-between times, he was able to provide his children with a first-class education!

The act was considered by some to be dangerous and risky and, indeed, it did not perform without the occasional incident. When appearing at the Alhambra Theatre of Varieties in West Hartlepool in April 1891, two of the children were involved in a minor accident:

The Selbini troupe of bicyclists and acrobats, having responded to an encore, were performing one of their most difficult and daring feats, when the two juvenile members, who were being rapidly borne round the stage suspended from a bar placed across the shoulders of the elder Selbini, who was mounted on a tall bicycle, suddenly lost their hold and fell to the stage. The youngsters seemed stunned for a moment, but they were soon on their feet again, and completed the act amidst a tremendous round of applause.

Of course, the Selbinis were not the only novelty bicycle act performing on the stage. The following acts were all advertising in *The Era* [Variety trade paper] on the twenty-third day of January 1892:

- Nick Kaufmann[35], billed as *Champion Cycle Trick Rider of the World* was appearing at the London Pavilion.

[35] Jack Selbini and Nick Kaufmann were considered by many to be the

- The Villions (the rival act set up by William Villion, Jack's partner in the Selbini and Villion Troupe), billed as *Combination Bicycle Acrobats, Twisting, Tumbling, Juggling, etc* were appearing with Ginnett's Circus in Norwich.
- French's Troupe, billed as *Bicyclists, Monocyclists, and Skaters* (five in number) were appearing at the Philharmonic in Cardiff.
- The Three Wonderful Paddocks, billed as *Champions of All Young Lady Trick Bicyclists*, were appearing with Keith's Circus in Bedford.

Jack believed that his troupe was the best in the world. Indeed, there was no shortage of bookings and he was able to demand high fees for appearances. Now that his daughter, Lalla (twelve years old at the beginning of 1891), was an experienced artiste, he threw out yet another challenge:

Talented Lalla Selbini, the greatest female trick rider in the world. Lalla is open to challenge any female trick rider, big or small, for £500.

No doubt, Jack would have had a successful career as a solo artiste but it is debatable whether he would have found international fame without the inclusion of his family into the act, especially the novelty of introducing his children at a young age. It is clear from newspaper reports at the time that the children tended to get a special mention wherever the troupe performed. During their career, the children received a number of awards from grateful theatre owners and managers. For example:

---

pioneers of trick cycling (and, apparently, Professor "Old Jock" Brown). From an early age, Lalla's cycling skills had been compared to Kaufmann's.

- In February 1886, Lalla and Leola Selbini were presented with two massive medals by M. Melville of the Grand Theatre in Birmingham.
- In April 1891, two massive gold medals were presented to Lalla and Willie Selbini by Messrs Moss and Thornton[36]. At the same ceremony, Victor Selbini was presented with a gold medal by the Magpie Cycling Club of Newcastle. An advertisement was placed in The Era on the ninth day of May to acknowledge the awards: *"The SELBINIS take this opportunity of thanking Messrs Moss and Thornton for their kind presentation of two massive gold medals to Miss Lalla and Master Willie Selbini on Thursday evening, April 30th; also thanking the members of the Magpie Cycling Club of Newcastle, for their kind reception, also for the handsome gold medal they presented to Victor Selbini, the merry little Magpie clown."*
- At the end of 1891, Director Mellini, of the Reichschallen in Cologne, presented a gold watch and chain, and many baskets of flowers and wreaths to Lalla Selbini.

Jack continually developed and enhanced the act in order to remain at the top of his profession. As his children grew older, he made their contribution to their shows more challenging and spectacular. In addition to cycling and tumbling, he introduced music, played simultaneously with riding, balancing, and leaping about the stage and he added humour through his [adopted] son Victor who played a clown. In 1894, he took out a patent on *Improvements in apparatus for stage and other public performances* to maintain the uniqueness of the troupe.

---

[36] Edward Moss and Richard Thornton owned a number of music halls in the north-east of England.

By 1894, the troupe had grown to eight members; Jack, his wife, his three daughters, his son, and two young men[37]. Lalla was a star attraction herself and she demonstrated exceptional skill as a bicyclist. One reporter stated, when reviewing a new act:

We can speak with sincere admiration of the Bale troupe of bicyclists. Avoiding comparisons as much as possible, we may say that they do not attempt any of the surprising feats of skill with which the graceful little girl of the Selbini troupe has made us familiar.

Lalla and Jack in 1896
(Source: London & Provincial Entr'Acte, November 28, 1896)

Even though the troupe was very busy with constant touring, Jack still found time to support charitable events. For example, in 1891, the troupe performed in the *Charles Morton*[38]

---

[37] The two men were William and Fred Etoile, although Fred was soon to leave the act. By the end of March 1894, Fred advertised for work, having left the troupe.

Testimonial Fund Matinee show at the Alhambra Theatre in Leicester Square and they performed for free at the Crystal Palace over the Whitsun holiday. No doubt, Jack believed that the publicity would enhance their standing in the theatrical world. He also made contributions to various charities such as the *Music Hall Benevolent Fund,* of which he was a member of the committee. Jack was an early member of the *Grand Order of Water Rats*, the charitable organisation of [male] music hall artistes and managers, which was established in 1889 to provide funds for the more needy, especially fellow artistes who had fallen on hard times.

In addition to the support for charities, Jack and his family were keen supporters of cycling as both a pastime and a sport. Many cycling clubs were appearing across the country in the 1880s and 1890s. Hengler's circus formed its own cycle club in 1890 which Jack participated in when he toured with them. Indeed, it may be that he was the driving force behind its creation although Albert Hengler, the proprietor of the circus, was the club captain. The club members often took to the roads on their bicycles in between shows, probably in order to promote the circus as well for the pleasure of cycling. Their first outing (in which Jack took part in) was reported in *The Era* on the twenty-second day of March 1890:

---

[38] Charles Morton was an impresario who established the first purpose-built music hall, the Canterbury, in 1852. Prior to that time, acts performed in taverns. He was known as the *Father of the Halls*. He announced his retirement in 1891 and the matinee was put on to celebrate the event (and to raise money for charity). Over fifty acts performed on the day, so their performances were limited to about five minutes each. In the programme, the audience were requested to not call for encores due to the limited time!

The Hengler's Circus Cycle Club, headed by their captain Mr A H Hengler, had their first outing from Birmingham on Tuesday last, wheeling to Stonebridge, via Solihull and Hampton. The party having lunched at the George Hotel, Solihull, and the health of the captain having been toasted with enthusiasm, the journey was continued, the pace-making being left to Mr Hengler, who brought his party on at a rapid speed, returning to town after completing a circular journey of twenty-five miles in three hours and a-half.

The National Cycle Show was organised by the major cycle manufacturers to exhibit their products. The Selbinis made a guest appearance at the third National Show in December 1894 and they were billed so: *"The celebrated and unrivalled Selbini troupe of bicyclists are specially engaged to appear in their remarkable and sensational track and comic riding feats."* By this time, cycling was a major pastime in Great Britain. The industry was employing between 75,000 and 100,000 people and there were about half a million members of cycling clubs.

In the early days of their career, the Selbinis travelled extensively with circuses and they had no permanent address. While on tour, they took up lodgings in a number of boarding houses. Eventually, they settled in London and, at the height of their success, in 1896, Jack bought a house, called Venetian Villa, at 193 Brixton Hill, for £1800. It was a substantial property and, according to the 1911 census, it contained eleven rooms (not counting the hallways, bathrooms, and scullery). The family was not in residence at the time of the 1901 census, the only occupiers being the gardener and his wife who were probably acting as caretakers. The Selbinis were possibly on tour again, perhaps in Europe. Jack sold the property on to Charles Austin (real name Parker Reynolds) who was also in the entertainment business.

The following article, which appeared in the *The Inquirer and Commercial News* in Australia on the tenth day of July 1896, sums up why the Selbinis remained successful for so long:

In these days of keen rivalry, originality and novelty are absolutely necessary to success, and to achieve that end one must keep abreast, if not ahead of the times. Especially is this fin-de-siècle[39] characteristic apparent in the world of pleasure, where the blasé amusement-seeker continually demands something novel to tickle his jaded palate. It is a testimony to the foresight and discernment of Mr. Selbini, the father of the clever troupe of trick-riders now appearing at various London West-End music-halls nightly, that his family of cyclists is as popular with the pleasure-seeking public of to-day as it was twenty-seven years ago[40]. It has always been admitted that, owing to its erratic propensities, the modern safety bicycle has not lent itself to trick-riding. Miss Lalla Selbini has overcome this difficulty, however, and her safety act is now one of the most attractive items on the Selbini programme. The performance is a very daring one, and very handsome does Miss Selbini look in her neat rational costume.

---

[39] Literally meaning "end of the century"; meaning *of, relating to, characteristic of, or resembling the late 19th-century literary and artistic climate of sophistication, escapism, extreme aestheticism, world-weariness, and fashionable despair.*

[40] The paper reported "twenty-seven years" but the original act of Villion and Selbini was formed in 1876 and Lily joined in 1879 – seventeen years before the article was published.

The troupe returned to Europe in 1896 where they were big attractions. They had appeared before the Crown Prince of Austria, and the King and Queen of Spain. This tour was the prelude to a major new undertaking by the family; a tour of Australia. The tour was organised by Harry Rickards, an English comic singer who settled in Australia and who owned theatres in a number of major cities. The Selbinis were the star attraction of the company that had been put together for the tour. The family set sail for Australia on the twenty-sixth day of February 1897 on board the P&O liner, the *SS Oceana*, and they arrived in Sydney on the eight day of May 1897, a journey of nearly two and a half months.

Their first engagement was at the Tivoli Theatre in Sydney, owned by Harry Rickards, on the fifteenth day of May 1897 and they were a big success. They received extensive coverage in the local newspapers. The following article appeared in the *Sydney Morning Herald* on the seventeenth day of May:

The fact that cycling, both as a sport and a means of locomotion, has come to stay will extend the interest taken in the marvellous performance introduced by the Selbini Troupe at the Tivoli Theatre on Saturday. Almost everyone nowadays can appreciate the difficulty of the bicycle tricks indulged in by the sportive amateur at athletic meetings. It must be admitted, however, that this act does not assist the spectator to understand in the least how these new wizards of the wheel maintain their equilibrium. Their feats are simply astounding in their sensationalism and as the element of grace is never absent, the Selbini cycle act forms the strongest and the strangest turn of its kind yet seen here. The new troupe consists of eight people[41], five of them acrobats of the first rate who throw furious somersaults of a weird character, one startling feat in this direction being a somersault which neatly clears the leader as he cycles slowly round the stage. Some of the most surprising feats are performed by the ladies of the troupe, athletes of perfect physique and great natural grace. The Selbini turn is very rapidly managed, the scarlet Mephistophelian costumes with spangles are alike, and it is somewhat difficult for a stranger to disentangle Mrs Selbini from her daughter - the case being indeed, one of "filia pulchra mater pulcherior" [beautiful mother, beautiful daughter]. But if recollection serves, it is the former who plays the mandolin while riding one wheel. Loud cheers greeted these feats. The audience was also delighted at the silver bar turn, the said bar being held between two bicyclists, who move slowly along while supporting the performer, and roars of laughter greeted the tall Selbini who pedalled round the stage on a wheel some eighteen inches high. One Selbini rode a single wheel built so much out of "plumb" that at every revolution the bulging portion struck the ground with a thump. Another coiled himself up within the circumference of a wheel and rolled himself swiftly round the stage in it. This feat was received with a fusillade of cheers and, in fact, we expect to see these clever people, sent here by Mr Harry Rickards as his 27th instalment of English artists, help to crowd the Tivoli for a long time to come.

---

[41] The troupe consisted of Jack and Lily, their four children, William and another unknown acrobatic. Unfortunately, the passenger lists for their journey to Australia do not identify the individuals; they are recorded as Mr Selbini, Messrs Selbini x3, Mrs Selbini, and Misses Selbini x3.

The troupe continued at the Tivoli for the next six weeks. Their act was called "the Satanic Gambols" and it included one particularly difficult trick, known as the "full spread", which Jack stated that he would no longer perform after they completed their Australian tour because of the physical strain it put on him:

With his two daughters held out at arm's length, and two men hanging onto his body, Jack rides an ordinary machine around the stage, finally bringing it to a standstill, and remaining stationary with his heavy burden for a period of about twenty seconds. The difficulties surrounding the feat can be the better appreciated when the gradual slope of the stage towards the footlights is borne in mind, so that nearly the whole of the work – steering, balancing and back-pedalling - is done by the feet.

The tour moved on to the Opera House in Melbourne, another theatre owned by Harry Rickards, where they opened on the third day of June. The Selbinis received further excellent reviews from the press. The article in the *Argus* on the fifth day of June was full of praise:

In these days, when everyone rides a wheel, the lot of the artist who endeavours to give trick displays on the bicycle is indeed hard. Such a show is now exposed to the view of the keenest critics, and tricks which four or five years ago would have been hailed as extraordinary are now howled down with derision by a populace which has seen far more extraordinary gyrations performed with no other properties than a borrowed "safety" and a greasy tramway line. Thus it was that the Selbinis, who on Saturday night made their first appearance at the Opera House, had to face a double risk. It was not alone that their performance needed to be excellent. The slightest error would have condemned them in the eyes of an audience of which nearly every man was a cyclist, and consequently was a critic. But the Selbini troupe did more than satisfy popular expectations. Never before has any trick bicyclist shown complete a mastery over the free and unfamiliar wheel. Like all trick bicyclists, the Selbinis display a preference for a form of the old "ordinary"[the penny-farthing], and the manner in which they rode this awkward machine – as it appears to modern ideas – round a limited stage, was enough to make the hair of any cyclist stand erect. But one of the two ladies proceeded to deliberately take her bicycle to pieces as she rode round the stage, concluding by standing on the pedals of the front wheel without even the fork crown to aid her, and in this dangerous position rode round and round with surpassing ease and grace, the enthusiasm of the audience could not be restrained. Among the other feats of the performance was a species of human Eifel Tower in which three of the troupe, standing on each other's shoulders, pedalled round the stage, followed by one of the ladies of the company, who, riding a "safety" [forerunner of the modern bicycle] in an extremely narrow circle, played a pretty mandolin accompaniment in time to the race, for race it was. To say what else the troupe did is hardly possible. They threw somersaults over each other's heads while careering at what the League of Victorian Wheelmen would term a "25-mile bat". They rode side-saddle, standing up in the saddle, on their heads, and in every conceivable and inconceivable way. They rode backwards, and they rode front ways, they flew up and down the stage on one bicycle that looked as though it had been struck by a locomotive, and that at every revolution, came down with the thump of a pile-driver; and finally they left the stage amid such a tumult of applause as has seldom been seen in a Melbourne theatre.

The company continued performing at the Opera House for the next ten weeks or so before returning to the Tivoli in Sydney at the end of August for another six weeks. The Selbinis were scheduled to return to England on the twenty-fourth day of October but, owing to their success, Harry Rickards negotiated a four-week extension. This last month was spent at the Theatre Royal in Adelaide. Jack and Lily's daughter, Mizpah, who was now eleven years old, was given her own solo spot and she was billed as the *Child Wonder of the World*. The enthusiasm and praise for the Selbinis from the Australian press continued unabated. The Adelaide newspaper, *The Advertiser*, reported on the third day of November:

Mr. Harry Rickards' Premier Vaudeville Company made their second appearance at the Theatre Royal on Tuesday evening, when they met with another enthusiastic reception. The marvellous performance of the Selbinis, which is not inappropriately styled "Satanic gambols on wheels" again took the house by storm, their entertainment being as original as it is daring, each member of the company performing a succession of feats while whirling round the stage which cannot fail to astonish the spectators. The juggling feats of the leader are performed with unerring dexterity, while the graceful exposition of fancy riding given by one of the ladies is one of the features of the exhibition. Every member of the combination is an acrobat, and the various feats are accomplished with such ease and grace as to make the performance a truly remarkable one. Mizpah, the child wonder, performed a series of marvellous feats on a blender wire and met with an enthusiastic reception.

The Australian tour finally came to an end and the Selbini family embarked on the liner the *SS Victoria* on the seventeenth day of November 1897, arriving back in England at the turn of the New Year. The Australian tour was probably the climax of their career. Although they were booked for engagements until about 1901, the act was about to undergo some major changes.

The Selbinis – Swan Song

William Selbini, who had been with Jack for many years as an apprentice, was now twenty-one years old and, having completed his apprenticeship, he left the troupe as soon as they had returned from Australia. Jack immediately advertised for a replacement.

The troupe remained in Great Britain throughout 1898, undertaking engagements in Derby, London, Newcastle, Edinburgh, Blackpool, Cardiff, and Nottingham. They continued to be the star attractions.

The family undertook another continental engagement at the beginning of 1899. They arrived in Germany in February of that year and they performed at the Mellini theatre in Hanover until Easter. They remained the star attraction:

This month of March brought an ensemble to the Mellini theatre which contains several splendid numbers. To the variety nobility the famous Selbini family belong. They are seven in number, and their wondrous performance, combined with splendid costumes, elegant work, and humorous tricks, again gave evidence that they are the best professional bicyclists in the world. Breathless, one follows every trick, and involuntarily one has to join in the stunning applause which shakes the house. The bicycle performance of the Selbinis has been brought to an incredible perfection on bicycles in full speed. They do gymnastic and juggling acts. The wheels are taken asunder piece by piece, so that at the finish only the front wheel remains, the lady carrying in her hand the hind wheel, saddle, and handle-bar while she continually pursues her way. The great talent of the Selbinis is combined with the faultless elegance and noblesse of their appearance. One young lady [Lalla] especially is in every respect a real pearl to the speciality theatre.

The troupe returned to England and undertook an engagement at the London Pavilion in June 1899. But the next major change in personnel was about to occur. Lily announced her retirement. An article appeared in *The Era* on the first day of July 1899:

Our readers will hear with regret that Mrs J Selbini, long associated with the triumphs of the celebrated Selbini troupe of bicyclists, had made up her mind to retire from the stage. Though she is the mother of grown up boys and girls, the popular bicyclist looks wonderfully young. She, however, thinks her husband and her girls and boys are quite capable of carrying on the business without her. She is the daughter of Kate Chatters, a popular and versatile actress, dancer, and pantomimist, and married Jack Selbini, whom she met in Germany, when she was scarcely eighteen. Mrs Selbini will be followed in her retirement by the regard and esteem of a large circle of professional and private friends. She will make her last appearance on Saturday, the 15th inst, at the Metropolitan. Mrs Selbini, who has been almost all her life connected with the halls, commenced her career as a characteristic vocalist and dancer.

The rest of the family continued with their busy schedule but they were now spending a lot more time in London. Over the following twelve months, they performed at the Paragon, Canterbury, New Bedford, and Oxford theatres in London as well as performing at the Crystal Palace. They also found time to perform in Portsmouth and Hastings. In spite of the busy schedule, Jack found time to support a number of social events at the beginning of 1900. He attended the annual dinner of the Grand Order of Water Rats in February. He was accompanied by his daughter, Lalla, rather than his wife, Lily. Perhaps Lily was indisposed or, perhaps, he wanted to promote Lalla and the dinner was an opportunity for her to meet influential people in show business. Jack also attended a farewell dinner for Paul Merinetti, a fellow artiste who was going on tour to Australia, and he attended the Music Hall Benevolent Fund dinner. He obviously enjoyed socialising! In September 1899, an American newspaper reported that George Lederer, a music hall manager and producer, had secured the "Selbini troupe of bicyclists and saxophonists" for a tour of America. However, there is no evidence that the troupe undertook such a tour. It may be that Lederer signed William Selbini because he [William] went to America after he left the troupe.

Following their season in London, the troupe continued touring the provinces, visiting Morecombe, Blackpool, Birkenhead, Manchester, Bolton, Bristol, and Plymouth. They still received good reviews, and the audiences were as enthusiastic as ever:

A speciality that is heartily enjoyed is the trick cycling of the Selbinis, a combination hard to beat on the wheel. Like a veritable fairy, the beautiful Miss Lalla Selbini careers round on a safety, accomplishing at will all kinds of tricks, and there is plenty acrobatic work, hat spinning, and mandolin strumming to vary the turn.

They undertook a further tour of the Continent at the beginning of 1901, appearing in France and Germany before returning to London in May.

The troupe appeared at Cheltenham at the Opera House in a pantomime *Little Red Riding Hood* which ran for about six weeks over the 1901 Christmas period. The pantomime gave one of the performers, Ernest Selbini[42], the opportunity to have a comic part in the pantomime as "the poodle". The pantomime moved to the Theatre Royal in Bath in January 1902 for further shows. The newspaper reviews for the Selbinis continued to be positive:

The poodle is cleverly represented by Master Selbini. This little fellow is one of a clever troupe of trick cyclists, who do a speciality turn. The Selbinis alone are worth a visit to the theatre, many of their feats being astounding in their cleverness.

However, a further change to the line up of the troupe was about to take place. Lalla Selbini left the act to marry and establish herself as a solo performer. Jack, Victor, Mizpah and Leola, remained in the troupe and the numbers were enhanced from time to time with other acrobats and cyclists. Lalla had become the star performer before her marriage and Jack now began to promote his other daughters, Leola and Mizpah, by giving them solo spots.

In spite of the changes in personnel, the Selbinis continued to be very busy but they were now almost exclusively performing in provincial theatres across Britain appearing in

---

[42] Ernest had been added to the troupe after they returned from their Australian tour.

Sunderland, Hastings, Bristol, Manchester, Dundee, Nottingham, Ardwick, and Hull over the next two years. In 1906, they were invited to be the chief attraction for the Whit Monday Fete at Leamington for a fee of £35[43]. They had not lost any of their skills and they still continued to receive favourable reviews, as reported in the Leamington newspaper following their appearance at the fete:

The Selbinis, the world-famed trick cyclists, followed, and to many present their performance was the principle feature of the programme. They are certainly well-versed in the tricks of the trade and their skill in handling the cycle came in for round after round of applause. Each member of the troupe displayed considerable ability, and the various manoeuvres they went through were followed with keen interest.

Mizpah left the troupe to get married in 1907 and she then pursued a solo career until teaming up with Archie Royer (see later).

Bicycle acts had now become established in the variety theatres and Jack continued to enhance his own act to ensure that the Selbinis remained the best. One trick was to perform a complete somersault while riding a bicycle and he added acrobatics on roller skates. Jack was now over fifty years old and he retired from performing in about 1909 although I have failed to find a formal announcement in any newspaper. However, he continued to lead the troupe but he left it to the younger male members to perform the difficult tricks.

---

[43] Earning £35 in 1906 is equivalent to earning £12,000 in 2013; not bad for a day's work!

The troupe continued performing their act in British theatres for many more years although there were now only four or five members. They continued to remain very popular with audiences. On the thirty-first day of October 1910, a poll of London's Evening News readers disclosed that the act were their favourite "Number 5" spot in an ideal Music Hall programme[44]. The troupe had arranged another continental tour, visiting Germany and Austria-Hungary but the outbreak of the First World War in 1914 caused the tour to be cancelled. The act was subsequently billed as an "artistic cycle pot pourri in black and white". In 1916, the troupe performed in Nottingham and an article appeared in the *Nottingham Evening Post* on the first day of April 1916, summarising the forty years of the Selbinis career. The following quote is from that article:

THE PIONEER TRICK CYCLISTS

For a troupe of trick cyclists to be able to boast of over 40 years' popularity is a wonderful record, and there is no wonder that the Selbinis are proud of it. Mr Jack Selbini, the father of the present members of the troupe, and one of the most remarkable veteran athletes of my acquaintance, was practically the originator of trick cycling, his only rival being Professor Brown, who was also known by the less dignified appellation of "Old Jock Brown." Mr Selbini started as a horse rider in Powell and Clarke's Circus, Londonderry and

---

[44] The full programme was 1: Overture; 2: Queenie Essex, comedienne; 3: Sandford and Lyons, comedians and dancers; 4: Alice Hollander, vocalist; 5: the Selbinis, trick cyclists; 6: King and Benson, comedy duo; 7: Little Tich, comedian; 8: Gertie Gitana, comedienne; 9: George Robey, comedian; 10: Ella Retford, comedienne; 11: Charles Austin and co. in sketch "Parker P.C."; Bioscope.

stuck to that line for about five years, when he was impressed by the possibilities of trick cycling, and started practising at once. His first machine was of the old-fashioned bone-shaker type, with wooden frame and iron-tyred wheels, which had to be roughened with a chisel to prevent them from slipping on the stage.

The Selbini Troupe in "Black and White"
(Image courtesy of *yorkshirebidding*)

The photograph above is from about 1915. The individuals are not named but by comparing the photograph with one of the troupe taken about five years earlier and with the photograph of the troupe taken in 1894, my best guess is that one of the men is Victor (possibly the one on the right), the older woman is Leola, and the young clown is Ernest. I cannot guess the names of the other two people.

There are no reviews or advertisements for the Selbini troupe beyond 1917. Other acts used the Selbini name after this date. For example, there was a troupe of female dancers in the 1930s who were billed as the *Selbini Girls*.

Lily and Jack retired to Thornton Heath in Surrey. In 1911, Lily had undergone and survived a serious operation for what was reported as "internal trouble". Perhaps she had a hysterectomy. She died on the third day of September 1930 at the Shrubland Nursing Home in Croydon. She was seventy years old. Her estate was valued at just over £952. Jack survived his wife by two years and he died on the fifth day of November 1932 at the age of seventy-eight years. His obituary in *Variety* magazine stated that he died in a London sanatorium of "a number of complicated ailments" but his probate record stated that he died at home. His estate was valued at just over £3378 [equivalent to about £200,000 in 2012].

The Selbinis – The Legacy

William Selbini

William in 1894 (Source: The Sketch, October   17, 1894)

William was born William Andrea Prati in London on the sixth day of September 1875, the son of Andrea Prati, an Italian equestrian performer, and Agnes Fraser, his Scottish wife. He was baptised at the St Nicholas Catholic Church in Liverpool on the sixteenth day of January 1876. William became articled to Jack Selbini although it is unclear when his apprenticeship began. It was possibly just after the troupe returned from their American tour of 1887 to 1889. He completed his apprenticeship with Jack and his final appearance with the troupe was on their tour of Australia in 1897. He had by then assumed the name of William Selbini and, as soon as he returned from Australia, he advertised for work:

WANTED. To join a first-class troupe or partner, Willie Selbini of the Selbini troupe. First class tumbler, mounter, and good musician. Can start immediately.

100

Jack advertised for a replacement at the same time. It is unclear whether William's departure from the troupe was amicable or not although I suspect that William, now an adult and having completed his apprenticeship, simply wanted to carve out a career of his own. Besides, Jack would have had to increase his wages! There is no evidence that William obtained a position in England following his advertisement but, a year later in about 1899, he travelled to America where he initially established a solo career as [the great] Selbini[45], performing as a trick cyclist and acrobat. The first record of an appearance in America that I have found is at Howard's Athenaeum in Boston in December 1901.

William soon teamed up with Lew Watson, a comic, to provide a bit more variety in his act, but their partnership, although successful, was short-lived. The main reason that they parted company was the fact that William married Julia Jane Grovini, known as Jennie or Jeanette, on the eighteenth day of January 1903 and William and Jennie decided to perform together. Jennie was born in England in 1874, the daughter of James Grovini, a clown who had a successful stage career in England for many years.

---

[45] Was William taking a liberty calling himself *The Great Selbini* or was the label given to him by the theatre managers, perhaps believing that they had hired the original Selbini (Jack)? In 1899, George Lederer claimed that he had secured the Selbini troupe for an American tour. Perhaps it was William he had engaged.

Selbini and Grovini

(Image from the *New York Clipper*, April 25, 1903 courtesy of Illinois
Digital Newspaper Collections, University of Illinois.)

The novelty of William and Jennie's act was that Jennie played the anchor role while William was thrown about by her! George J. Richardson of the *Boston Traveller* newspaper described their act as following:

Wm. Selbini and Jennie Grovini are gifted at wholesale. They do acrobats of various sorts; juggle things and ride bicycles, both safety and of the high wheel variety, as if they had wings. The most curious feature is that the woman does all the heavy part of the acrobats, and throws the man about as if he was as a cushion. I wonder if he was her husband. [He was!] If so, the domestic ménage must be on an extremely settled basis.

William and Jennie settled in America where they had a successful career for well over twenty years. They were granted American citizenship on the twenty-second day of April 1920. However, they had to work hard and make sacrifices in the early years of their career in order to establish their act. A newspaper report in the *New York Sunday Telegraph* on the twelfth day of November 1905 illustrated some of the wheeling and dealing that was required to get engagements. It also illustrated the risks that were involved:

Selbini and Grovini got a good deal from the Jacobs & Lowery people. Rehearsed four weeks here, for which, of course, no coin came in; played the first week for half salary, on the dear old gag, "New show and won't do much business you know"; then worked nine weeks on the road, and were suddenly closed because their salary was too high. As they had put $600 into their acrobatic act, for new effects, platings, etc., expecting a full forty weeks work, they feel somewhat aggrieved. Selbini intends to start legal proceedings at once, suing on the contract which he claims was broken.

I do not know the outcome of the legal action.

Their act received mixed reviews but William was not short on confidence, perhaps something he learned from Jack. A review in Variety in 1906 described their act as:

"Nothing new in tumbling or bicycle riding, the feature is that Miss Grovini is the understander in all the work shown. Juggling while riding the wheel was the best of the work"

Whereas a review in the New York Clipper in 1907 stated:

"Selbini and Grovini are doing a phenomenal act of strength and agility, and create a stir everywhere they appear, in their tumbling acrobatics and unique bicycle feats, the lady doing all the understanding, making the onlookers marvel at some

of the feats they performed, little realizing the years of practice and hard work such tricks necessitate".

William and Jennie visited England on a couple of occasions; in 1907 for "business reasons" and in 1911, when they played at two London Music Halls, billed as the "Praties" [their real name].

Although they never reached the star billing that Jack Selbini's troupe had achieved, William and Jennie were constantly touring America for over twenty years, developing and refining their act over the years. A review of their performance in Duluth, Minnesota, stated:

One of the best acts on the bill is the athletic opening. William Selbini (with an English accent) and Jeanette Grovini open the bill in "Follies of Vaudeville" in which almost every athletic and trick act one ever sees on a bill is given. Miss Grovini is built like a piano mover but, nevertheless, is graceful and by no means slow of movement. She does the "strongman" act for the team, and has a remarkably good partner. Mr Selbini does the trick work, and does it well.

William and Jennie were booked to tour Australia in 1926 and they were due to set sail on the thirtieth day of December 1925. However, they had to cancel the tour due to Jennie suffering from rheumatism. She was about fifty years old at that time and, no doubt, her long career was beginning to take toll of her body. They did continue performing in America and embarked on a road show in early 1926, supported by Cronin and Hert, a song and dance duo; Ruso, Tele, and Ruso, an acrobatic act; Wood and White, a comedy duo; and the Four Phillips, jugglers and balancers. The road show was billed as THE SELBINI & GROVINI ROAD SHOW NUMBER 53, which illustrates just how busy they had been throughout their career. Details of the show were recorded in a poem written by Milt Wood, one of the acts, as a tribute to William and Jennie, and to celebrate their twenty-fourth wedding anniversary. An extract from the poem illustrated the relationship between William and Jennie:

> And they are still sweethearts, and this is a fact
> They always kiss each other every time they finish their act.
> If you want to enjoy happiness, you must earn it they say;
> If such is the case they should be supremely happy for many a day.
> We presented them with a silver loving cup inscrolled with the names of the show,
> And as the years go by, they will point to it by pride, I know.

The show may have been their last one as I have not found any reports on them after the tour.

William died at his home in Somerville, New Jersey on the twelfth day of September 1940. As soon as the Second World War ended, Jennie applied for a passport to travel to England. She arrived in Southampton on the twenty-fifth day of September 1945 and she went to live with her sister, Mrs Emily Lister, in Blackpool. She died of myocardial degeneration [heart disease] at her sister's house on the twelfth day of January 1955. She was eighty years old and she also suffered from dementia.

Lalla Selbini

Lalla Selbini in 1907

(Source: MyHeritage.com [online database]. Lehi, UT, USA: MyHeritage
(USA) Inc .San Francisco News Letter, July 1907)

Lalla, the eldest daughter of Jack and Lily, was born Mary
Elizabeth McCoy at Douglas on the Isle of Man on the
twenty-eighth day of August 1878. She started performing
with the Selbini troupe from the age of four years and she
remained a vital part of the act until 1902. As an adult, she
was considered one of the most beautiful women in show
business, and she achieved international fame, or as some
people considered it, infamy. Details of her life and career are
given later. She had an immediate impact when she went to
America, which is summed up by the entry on her in the
Actor's Birthday Book, published in 1908[46]:

---

[46] Courtesy of archive.org
(https://archive.org/details/actorsbirthdaybo02brisuoft)

A TALENTED and versatile girl is Lalla Selbini, she of the wondrous grace and beautiful face and figure. Her name has become a synonym for all the graces in woman's calendar, and a just homage, too, when one considers her youth, beauty and striking personality. Miss Selbini is one of the leading lights in the vaudeville world and she has won a position almost unique in itself by the originality and uncommon cleverness of her act. For a number of years she was a reigning favourite in all the foreign music halls and her name and following extended throughout England, France, Germany, Russia, South Africa, Egypt and Australia. It was the summer of 1906 that she made her bow before an American audience, appearing at Hammerstein's Victoria Roof Garden, being happily billed as " The Bathing Beauty," and so enormous was her vogue that she reigned triumphant throughout the entire summer, playing sixteen consecutive weeks, a run far greater than that enjoyed by any other performer. Since then she has toured all over the United States, playing the leading vaudeville houses from the Atlantic to the Pacific, and she proved the sensation of the hour in each city she visited. A woman of exceptional mental qualities, with a deep thirst for knowledge, Miss Selbini is a fluent linguist and is the mistress of four languages, though she even proposes to add to this number as time goes on. A further evidence of her grey matter, she composes all of her own songs, makes her gowns (and very handsome and striking they are, too), designs and paints her own scenery, and has complete charge and direction of her vaudeville offering. Her rightful claim to being a true daughter of Venus, Miss Selbini was selected as the model for all the decorations in the Manhattan Opera House. Small wonder she is called talented,

107

versatile and beautiful. Assured success is a fine thing in its way, but to a woman of Miss Selbini's mental calibre it merely acts as an incentive to achieving bigger things. She has won conspicuous note in her own particular line, and it is greatly to her credit that she is not content to rest satisfied with her present condition. Lalla Selbini is a worthy exponent of the modern-day woman of brains and ambition, and richly deserves all the success possible.

Victor Selbini

Victor in 1894
(Source: The Sketch, October 17, 1894)

Victor was born in Scotland in about 1881[47] and he was always referred to as the son of Jack and Lily. It may be that they saw Victor as a replacement for their son, Christopher, who died on his first birthday.

---

[47] According to *The Era*, Victor was born on February 26. This is the same birth date as Jack and Lily's son, Charles. It seems too much of a coincidence that Victor and Charles were born on the same day although Victor is not the same person as Charles. Charles' life is confirmed by a birth record for him in Glasgow, a newspaper article publicising his birth, a death record for him in Marylebone, and a death announcement in the press. Nor is there any evidence that Charles and Victor were twins.

Victor was introduced into the troupe in about 1889 to provide a comic touch. He was originally known as the *Merry Little Magpie Clown* and he became a big hit with the public. Like all members of the troupe, Victor was a skilled cyclist, usually performing on a monocycle. Victor appears to have remained loyal to Jack and he may have remained with the Selbini troupe until it disbanded in about 1918.

Victor retained the surname *Selbini* even though it was only his stage name. His wife's name was Clara Green although I have been unable to find a marriage record for them. They may have married abroad. Clara was born in Birmingham in about 1887, the daughter of West and Agnes Green. Victor and Clara lived in Tottenham in North London. They did not have any children.

Victor and Clara created their own cycling act in 1919 and billed themselves as the *Selbini Duo*. They appeared at the Wood Green Empire in August 1919 and a report appeared in *The Era* on the third day of September:

The clever cycling duo, Victor and Clara Selbini, made their reappearance in town at the Wood Green Empire last week, meeting with great favour. They are now in the provinces for a while, returning to London at the Victoria Palace early in October.

Victor and Clara performed in variety theatres for about the next five years although they failed to make any significant impact. The newspaper articles of the period do not describe their act in any detail and there are no extensive reviews.

Victor died at the age of fifty-seven years and his death was registered in Edmonton between April and June 1938. Clara survived Victor by nearly thirty years and she died at the age of about eighty years. Her death was registered at Hinckley in the county of Leicestershire between January and March 1967.

Leola Selbini

Leola in about 1905
(Source: Vintage Postcard)

Leola Lily McCoy, the second daughter of Jack and Lily, was born in Lowestoft in the county of Suffolk on the thirteenth day of August 1882. Her elder sister, Lalla, had been cared for in Lowestoft by a farmer, James Cooper, and his wife while Jack and Lily toured America. On their return, they rented accommodation in Lowestoft during Lily's confinement. Lily returned to performing with the family troupe just six weeks' after Leola was born.

Leola started performing with the rest of the family from the age of about three years and she was an instant success. In a review of the Selbini act when they were performing with Hengler's Cirque in Hull, dated the second day of October 1885, Leola and her sister received special praise:

But more astonishing still are the performances of Baby Lalla, truly called the infant phenomenon, and her little sister [Leola]. These little dots are aged five and three years respectively, and yet, young as they are, they are even cleverer then their parents, considering the differences in years. The feats which these two mites perform on bicycles, the driving wheels of which are about a foot and a foot and a half in diameter, are very similar to those mentioned above, and the house is fairly brought down when the younger one is placed in a small wheelbarrow and is wheeled quickly round by her little sister, seated on her bicycle.

Leola was due to travel with the family on their American tour of 1887 to 1889 but she suffered ill health. She had chronic bronchitis, and one of her lungs was affected. The doctors said it would hasten her death for her to continue in the business. As a consequence of her illness, she was placed into *The Sisters of Mercy Roman Catholic Convent* in Brighton for four years from 1887 to 1891. When she came out, Jack decided that she should try to perform again with the family troupe. After a couple of years, she gained in weight and strength, and was completely free from her lung infection. Jack believed that it was his strict training regime that he subjected his children to that helped her to recover quicker. In an interview that he gave to a reporter in 1893 when the troupe were performing at the Empire theatre in Cardiff, to the question *"What are the physical effects of your training?"*, he said in response:

"Oh, most beneficial. For instance, my daughter, who was in a convent for four years, and at the time of her removal there from, was certainly in a decline, after six months of my training was perfectly restored, and is now one of the healthiest girls in Great Britain, as you can see for yourself."

Just before the Selbinis embarked upon their tour of Australia in 1897, a public notice was placed in *The Era* announcing the engagement of Mr Henri French, a trick bicyclist, to Lola (sic) Selbini. Because the announcement misspelt the first name of the bride-to-be, it could be either Lalla, who was eighteen years old at that time, or Leola, who was fourteen years old, although it is more likely that it was Lalla.

However, it transpired that neither Lalla nor Leola married Henri although, in spite of the fact that the engagement was made public, there appears to have been no fallout.

Leola and Lalla in 1894
(Source: The Sketch, October 17, 1894)

Leola continued performing with the troupe and she married Victor James Harraway, in 1912, under the name of Leola L McCoy. The marriage was registered at Wandsworth between July and September. They had one daughter, Joan, who was born in Croydon on the ninth day of July 1917. Victor was an electrical engineer, running his own business in partnership with Archibald Cunningham. However, the advent of the First World War caused his business plans to be put on hold and he joined the Royal Navy Volunteer Reserve. He was the son of an army officer so he had a military upbringing. He transferred as a captain to the army in 1916 and he had a distinguished career, being mentioned in despatches twice but he was invalided home. After he was demobilised from the army in 1919, he did not return to his former career but he and Leola decided to immigrate to Canada. The family arrived in

British Columbia on the twenty-third day of May 1920 to start a new life as farmers although, later, Victor joined the penitentiary service.

Leola died in British Columbia at the age of sixty-five years on the twelfth day of January 1948. Her death was reported in *Billboard* magazine on the thirty-first day of January as a reminder of her show business past:

SELBINI-Leo, former member of a well-known English bicycle act, the Selbini Family, January 12 in Ganges, B. C., Canada. Survived by a sister, Mizpah (Mrs. Archie Roger), Bangor, Michigan, USA.

Victor remarried and he died in British Columbia at the age of eighty-two years on the sixteenth day of May 1968.

Victor and Leola's daughter, Joan, firstly married Robert A Harrell and then she married Albert C Stadtegger. She died at the age of forty-seven years in San Mateo, California on the ninth day of April 1965.

Mizpah Selbini

(Source: Vintage postcard)

Mizpah Agnes McCoy, the youngest daughter of Jack and Lily, was born in Aston, Birmingham, on the fifteenth day of February 1886. When the Selbinis toured America in 1887, Mizpah was an infant and she did not travel with them.

Like her two older sisters, Mizpah started performing with the rest of the family from an early age. She was touring with the family by 1891. Her speciality in the troupe was to perform acrobatics on a horizontal bar being held by the male cyclists. I have failed to find any explicit references to her in the numerous newspaper articles until the family toured Australia in 1897. Now aged eleven years old, Jack billed Mizpah as the *Child Wonder of the World on the invisible wire.*

Mizpah married Roland Charles Gallier, a grocer's assistant, by license at Aston registry office on the twenty-sixth day of June 1907, under the name of Mizpah McCoy. Her siblings, Victor and Leola, were witnesses to the marriage. They signed their names "McCoy". Mizpah and Roland had a daughter, Patricia Lily whose birth was registered in Aston between October and December 1907.

In 1908, Mizpah accompanied her sister Lalla on her European tour but she failed to secure sufficient bookings for her solo act and she returned to her family. She and Roland had a second daughter, Eugenia May, known as Jean, who was born in London on the third day of May 1911.

After the birth of her second daughter, Mizpah teamed up with an American acrobat named Archie Royer and she re-launched her career, building upon her acrobatic skills rather than her cycle riding. The first reference that I have found for her act is from the *Dundee Courier* on the twenty-sixth day of November 1912:

The name Selbini stands for ability on the music-hall stage. Mizpah Selbini upholds the traditions of the name. Miss Selbini dances and juggles simultaneously, spins hats cleverly, and is an expert spade jumper. She also tumbles and somersaults with graceful ease. Miss Selbini is ably assisted by Mr Archie Royer, who is a wonderful performer for his years. Mr Royer is a slippery "youth" of 51! He is great as a high kicker, and his somersaults from the knee are marvellous.

According to an article published in the *Pottstown Mercury* in 2013, Archie was born Irvin Royer in Pottstown, Pennsylvania, on the fourteenth day of November 1869, the son of William Royer, a carpenter, and his wife Hannah. Archie was a natural acrobat and he supposedly ran away from home at an early age to join a circus. However, he returned to his home town and established his own show entitled "Next Door" which was described as a mixture of comical farce, pantomime, and an exhibition of tumbling and contortion. It featured his brothers and his first wife, Rose Zeigler whom he had married in 1893. Initially, the show was a success but tragedy struck early on in 1899 when Archie's wife Rose and his brother Eddie died. However, Archie resurrected the show and it continued running for another six years. During that time, Archie married three more times. His fourth wife, whom he married in 1904, was Mystya Ferol Steffan who was a trapeze artiste.

Early in 1905, the show was in difficulties due to poor attendances and Archie abandoned it in Illinois when he was part way through a tour. He returned with Mystya to her home town leaving eight members of the cast in Illinois with just three weeks' wages. The show was resurrected yet again and ran for a further two years but Archie then went solo, supported by Mystya. He secured a tour of Great Britain in 1908 and he was joined by his wife but, by this time, she was pregnant and did not perform with him.

Mystya gave birth to a son, Archie Jacques Edward Royer, in London soon after she arrived in England. Archie senior began touring England and the *Western Times*, a newspaper published in Devonshire, described his act in a review published on the third day of November 1908:

Archie Royer, a Yankee comedy acrobat, is quite above the ordinary, and some of his tricks we have never seen equalled for quickness and droll effect, while his magic-like knee somersaults have surely never seen attempted before. Royer is

117

a versatile little artist, with sufficient of the comedian's spirit to give a quaintly original touch to his exceptional acrobatic skill.

Archie had a small physique; standing at just five-feet and two-inches tall and weighing about nine stone but he had great strength which enabled him to perform his acrobatics. He remained in Great Britain for five years and, although he obtained a number of engagements, he failed to achieve star status even though he claimed in letters to America that he had top billing. When he teamed up with Mizpah Selbini, it was obvious that he was the support and the star of the act was Mizpah. Perhaps the relationship between Archie and Mizpah was initially professional, but it soon developed into an affair.

Meanwhile, his fourth wife, Mystya, appeared as Kit Larson in George Street's stage production of a western drama called "The Cattle Thief". The production appeared in theatres across England for a number of years. *Billboard* reported that Mystya achieved tremendous success in the role but she only appeared in the drama for a short time in 1913. Mystya returned to America where she remarried in 1916.

Within about a year of their teaming up, Archie returned to America with Mizpah, who now called herself Mizpah Royer, and his son Archie junior. They arrived in New York on the twenty-fourth day of February 1913. Mizpah's daughter, Patricia, later joined them, accompanied by a chaperone, Annie Davis, arriving in New York on the seventeenth day of August 1913. She travelled under the name of Patricia Royer and the passenger list stated that she was the daughter of

118

Archie and Mizpah. Mizpah's youngest daughter, Jean, joined the family the following year, arriving in New York on the second day of November 1914 with chaperones Alfred and Eliza Bland. Like her sister, she travelled under the name of Royer, the daughter of Archie. Mizpah's husband, Roland Gallier, moved to India where he was a store manager in Bangalore. He did not remarry and he died in the Bangalore hospital on the twenty-seventh day of February 1921 at the age of forty years.

Mizpah continued with her act in America, supported by Archie but she failed to achieve the same level of success that Jack, Lalla, or William had achieved there. Initially, their act was hyped up. For example, when they appeared in Washington in the summer of 1913, the local newspaper reported:

The Cosmos Theatre announces this week the special engagement of Mizpah Selbini and Archie Royer, two of vaudeville's celebrities, in a hodgepodge of unusually difficult feats of strength and skill. This act was one of the biggest hits in Western vaudeville circuits last winter, and comes to the Cosmos tomorrow afternoon for a first appearance in Washington.

MIZPAH SELBINI

Assisted By
ARCHIE ROYER
in Marvellous Feats
Of Strength & Skill.

(Source: The Washington herald. (Washington, D.C.), 30 Aug. 1913.
America: Historic American Newspapers)

Archie appears to have been an enigma. When he toured Great Britain, he wrote letters to the *Daily Pottstown Herald* claiming that he was a big success and, in his own words, *"I will never be home. I am booked in London for life"*. However, he was back in America a few years later, playing second fiddle to Mizpah. Another letter he wrote after his return to America praised English performers but maligned American ones. He criticised Canadians, advising English acts to *"Keep away from Canada"*. No doubt, he managed to make himself a number of enemies while others considered him eccentric.

Archie Royer junior, son of Archie and Mystya Steffon, died of spinal meningitis on the twenty-fifth day of March 1918 at the age of nine years. He was buried in Monks Cemetery in Bangor, Michigan. Mizpah and Archie senior were later interred in the same grave.

Archie bought a crop farm in Bangor, Michigan, and went into semi-retirement so he was no longer dependant on theatre bookings to earn a living. He and Mizpah finally married in Philadelphia on the fifteenth of February 1922 after Mizpah's husband, Roland Gallier, had died. Both Archie and Mizpah declared that they had never been married before! The 1920 US census claimed that Archie and Mizpah married in England in 1903 which, from other evidence, was clearly untrue. However, the "lie" enabled Mizpah to claim American citizenship through her American "husband".

Mizpah continued performing, supported by Archie, until about 1922 when they retired completely from the stage to concentrate on their farm. A newspaper report just before they retired described their performance as small time and only worthy as an opening act. Perhaps this criticism persuaded them to call it a day.

However, Archie could not totally abandon his show business life and he created a miniature circus with a cast ranging from equilibrists and clowns to educated white rats. Mizpah and her two daughters took part in the circus which performed at county fairs. The acts in the circus also included the Selbini Girls [sometimes called the Selbini Sisters]. When Archie died, his death announcement in Billboard stated that he had formed an act with "Mizpah Selbini and Lalla". Could Mizpah and Lalla have teamed up as the Selbini Girls? Lalla was still performing with her own act at the time but she may have made guest appearances with Archie's circus.

Patricia, Mizpah's eldest daughter, became a professional boxer, performing at the county fairs with Archie's circus, billed as "The Girl Jack Dempsey". When she appeared at the Van Wert county fair in 1928, the *Van Wert Daily Bulletin* reported on the twenty-second day of August:

One of the outstanding attractions to be offered is Patricia Royer, a noted boxer whose home is Bangor, Michigan, and whose age is 20 years. Patty Royer is a rarity among her sex – a boxer. She has fought seventy-five matches, of which seventy-one were exhibitions with men weighing anywhere from 125 pounds to 175 pounds. She has been matched against women five times, winning every bout. She earns with her fists, if her earnings can be computed separately from those of the rest of the Royer family, about $5,000 each year.

When she was twenty-five years old, Patricia retired from her boxing career and trained to be a salesperson. There is no mention of Patricia in Archie's death notice and she may have died before him.

Mizpah's youngest daughter, Jean, also appeared with the circus as "The Eugenie Climax – high aerial sensation". She married Elmer George Klobnak and she died on the sixth day of January 1983 at the age of seventy-one years. Elmer, who was seven years younger than Jean, died on the twenty-eighth day of May 1988.

In 1943, Archie wrote a letter to Walter Main, a circus owner, on the fiftieth anniversary of a train disaster that had hit the circus. Archie was performing with the circus at the time of the disaster. In 1955, the *Huntingdon Daily News* [Pennsylvania] carried an article recalling the train disaster and it included extracts from Archie's letter which are confusing. Archie stated in the letter that he and Mizpah had a daughter "dear little Rose who died in 1901" [Note: Archie's first wife. Rose, had died in 1899] and they "were blessed with another wonderful girl". But Archie did not meet Mizpah until about 1910 and she was only fifteen years old in 1901. Further, there is no evidence that Archie and Mizpah had any natural children, although Archie had adopted her two daughters from her first marriage. Did Archie suffer from dementia or did he simply get confused? After all, he had had five wives!

Mizpah recovered from a serious illness in 1944 but I do not have any details. She died just before her sixty-ninth birthday and she was buried at Bangor, Michigan, on the fourth day of February 1955. Archie died on the twentieth day of September 1956 at the age of eighty-six years.

Other Members of the Selbini Troupe
Apart from the McCoy family, a number of individuals joined the troupe from time to time. Some of them have already been identified in the earlier text and newspaper reports and advertisements have identified further individuals. William Prati (Willie Selbini) is covered in detail in a previous section. Other individuals are as follows.

Mademoiselle Jeanette, the accomplished, a female acrobat was part of the Selbini troupe in 1882 during its formative years.

J Alpha (male), a trick bicyclist and acrobat, joined the Selbini troupe in 1884 during their American tour. He was possibly an American.

Fred Etoile was part of the troupe in 1894 and he may have joined earlier than that year. He had left the troupe by March 1894 when he was advertising for work.

Ernest Allen Selbini joined the troupe in about 1900. When he appeared with them in 1902, he was referred to as "Master Selbini" so he was not an adult. He may have been another apprentice but there are few records for him.

The New York Clipper reported on the first day of August 1917 that **Lou and Will Dale**, late of the Selbini Troupe, were performing a new comedy bicycle act at the Osborne Theatre in Manchester. The act was billed as *Dale, Simkins, and Dale*. Lou and Will performed as a duo in 1918 but I have not found any other records for them in the British newspapers.

The Ruthin Garden Fete in 1906 featured "**Wheeler and Wilson**, members of the much talked about Selbini Troupe". I have not found any other references to the duo, who are not to be confused with the later father and son comedy duo of Wheeler and Wilson. It may be that the names were pseudonyms chosen for a one-off performance given that not all the members of the Selbini Troupe were performing at the fete; the names possibly refer to "wheels".

An obituary was published in 1929: **James Neagle**, 76, old time acrobat and contortionist who appeared under the name of **Mizano** died in London August 9. Many years ago, deceased was with the Selbini Troupe. His death was registered under the name of John Neagle so the newspaper may have reported his name incorrectly. I cannot find any other information about Mizano.

Another Willie (originally **Willie Selbini** but later **Willie Seltini**) joined the troupe in about 1900. The following article appeared in the *Nottingham Evening Post* on the twenty-seventh day of May, 1916:

THE SELTINIS

Years ago – not so may either – there were no regulations regarding the employment of child performers, who were "caught young", subjected to high-pressure training, and turned out as the finished article in an amazing short space of time. The system of unrestricted child exploitation was of course not commended, but it produced some of the cleverest acrobats and speciality artists of the present day, among them Willie Seltini, whose dancing and tumbling and somersault act on roller skates seems to leave very little else to be attempted in that direction. Mr Seltini, who is only a year or two over the 30 mark, has been a performer for 26 years, starting with a troupe called the Georgettis, with whom he worked the Continent, including Russia.

A fact of particular interest about Mr Seltini is that he was a member of the original Selbini trick cycling troupe. He was articled to Jack Selbini, the founder, and served an apprenticeship until he was 21. With the Selbinis he toured everywhere on the Continent, as well as the United Kingdom, and appeared several times before European Royalties with his roller-skating act.

For several years past, he has travelled his own troupe under the name of the Four Seltinis, but the war was the cause of the act being broken up, the men being claimed by the army. Mr Willie Seltini is himself an attested man but has twice been rejected on medical grounds, as his papers show. He has four brothers with the colours, of whom one has lost his leg, and another has been thrice wounded, and is just about to return to the front for the fourth time.

Assuming Willie joined the Selbinis at the age of 14 years, he would have been articles in about 1899 so he may have been a replacement for William Prati. However, he was still part of the troupe in 1909 when he went by the name of Willie Selbini. Of course, he may have stayed with the Selbinis after he completed his apprenticeship. The first reference to the Seltinis that I have found is when *Seltini and Vivian* performed at the Royal Hippodrome in Eastbourne in August 1913. The act soon evolved into the Selbini Trio, assisted by Lillias (or the Four Seltinis). But by the time of the Nottingham Evening Post article, Willie was performing as a duo billed as Willie and Charles Seltini, roller skating novelties. I have not found any information about the Georgettis.

In 1921, **Rollette** was advertising for work. He described himself as an "acrobat and dancer on skates, late of the Selbinis".

Part 3:

Lalla Selbini

(Source: The evening world. (New York, N.Y.), 06 June 1906. Chronicling America: Historic American Newspapers)

Early Life

Lalla was to become more famous than her parents. Coached by her father from an early age, she became a highly skilled cyclist but it was her beauty, which she inherited from her mother, and how she exploited it, that brought her the most fame.

As soon as she reached her fourth birthday, she started performing as part of the Selbini troupe, being billed as Baby Lalla, *"The smallest and cleverest baby bicyclist in the universe."*

Lalla, about 4 years old
(Source: Vintage postcard)

She toured with her parents in America but not without controversy when her father was charged with child cruelty! However, Lalla seems to have been a skilled performer at an early age and relished the spotlight, rather than being "forced" to perform by her parents. Her act was described in a report in the *Irish Times* on the ninth day of June 1885:

One of the members of this troupe, Baby Lalla, is a perfect example. The child, who is scarcely six years old, appears to take delight in performing difficult feats on the bicycle, and from beginning to end of her performance, she attracts to herself the attention of all her spectators. She is one of the cleverest and heartiest little creatures that ever performed before the public.

She began to receive medals for her performances and she was billed as "the wonder of the universe". By the time she was ten years old, she was described as "the most expert juvenile bicycle rider in the world" and her performance was compared to that of Kaufmann. [Note: Nicholas Edward Kaufmann was a Swiss-American who was unofficial world champion in artistic cycling in 1888].

By the age of thirteen years, the public was becoming aware of her developing beauty as a young woman as well as her now well-established cycling skills. She was being described as "Beautiful little Lalla", "Cupid of the wheel", and "graceful". In January 1892, the Selbinis agent, Warner, threw out a challenge to all-comers:

Talented LALLA, the greatest female trick rider in the world. Lalla, Lalla, Lalla is open to challenge any female trick rider, big or small, for £500.

Lalla at the age of 16
(Source: The Sketch, October 17, 1894)

As an adult, Lalla was a petite five feet tall, with dark hair, brown eyes, and a voluptuous figure. Not surprisingly, she was beginning to attract admirers and suitors. It was probably Lalla who was engaged to Henri French before the family set off on their tour of Australia. Lalla attended a ball in Hanover when the Selbinis were on a continental tour in early 1897 and she was showered with gifts.

Pretty Lalla Selbini has conquered Hanover. At the Mellini ball, Count Konigsmark said she was the loveliest girl in the ballroom, and she has been the admired of all Hanover during the past month. She has been the recipient of many valuable presents, amongst them being a beautiful little gold watch from the proprietors of the theatre, a massive gold bracelet from Count Konigsmark, a gold bicycle brooch and a dressing case with ivory-backed brushes, etc, and a diamond brooch, wreaths and baskets of flowers innumerable from other admirers, and she has been invited to some of the finest families in Hanover. Papa and Mamma Selbini, who have

131

also been the recipients of floral gifts, have reason to be proud of their lovely girl.

When the family returned from their Australian tour, Lalla escorted her father on a number of social events. Whether this was because Lily was incapacitated or whether it was an excuse for Jack to find Lalla a husband is open to debate. She took part in competitive cycling. In 1898, she came second in the *One Mile Ladies' Bicycle Handicap* race, behind Ada Dell, who was also on the stage. The race was an annual charity event in aid of the Music Hall Benevolent Fund. In 1900, Lalla was presented with a silver jewellery cask by the editor of *Gaiety* for being voted the most beautiful woman in variety theatre.

Lalla, no doubt with help from her father, developed her own unique act. The best description of the act appeared in a review of the Selbinis in the *Sydney Morning Herald* in 1897 when they toured Australia:

Miss Selbini rides upon one wheel round the stage backwards as well as forwards. The youthful athlete also balances herself on the pedals of the machine when it is upside down working the wheel at full speed and allows one of the company to throw a somersault from her shoulders without deviating from the circuit her wheels are pursuing. Loud cheers greeted this statuesque looking maiden when she took her bicycle to pieces while riding round, until at last she bestrode the wheel without handles or steering gear of any kind - just the one wheel with pedals.

But a big change was about to occur in Lalla's life. She married Willy Pantzer in Lambeth, London, on the eighteenth day of March 1902. The wedding was reported on in detail in *The Era* on the twenty-second day of March:

Two celebrated families of gymnasts have become related by the life contract entered into on Tuesday by Mr William Pantzer and Miss Lallah Selbini, whose wedding has created a great deal of interest in variety circles. The bride is so well known to the profession that it is hardly necessary to say that she is the second (sic) daughter of Mr "Jack" Selbini, who has for many years been associated with the triumphs of the Selbini Troupe of bicyclists and acrobats in all parts of the world. Miss Lallah indeed has known no other tutor or entrepreneur than her father and mother, and her grace, beauty, and cleverness, we do not hesitate to say, have won the admiration of thousands of variety lovers in both hemispheres. The bridegroom belongs also to a family celebrated in the annals of the variety stage, and has attained, with his brother, Mr Ernest Pantzer, a high reputation as a gymnast. He is tall, fair, and handsome, and the bride has the dark hair and blue eyes which are typical of the Irish race, to which she belongs.

The article went on to give details of the ceremony, the show business and family guests, and the presents that were given and received. The guest list included Captain Flowerday, Aunt Agnes, and Aunt Kate. Agnes and Kate were Lily Selbini's sisters but there is no mention of her brother William. He was performing with the Brothers Lorenzi and Sisters Phillips at the time so he possibly had other commitments.

Willy Pantzer

Willy Pantzer from his passport application in 1916
(Courtesy of Ancestry.co.uk)

Willy was born Heinrich Louis Carl Wilhelm Pantzer in Dortmund, Germany, on the eighth day of August 1872, the eldest son of Charles Pantzer and Eliza Jones. The Pantzers were a noble German family, having been raised to the peerage in 1438 for their support of King Albert II [known as Albert the Magnanimous]. However, Willy's grandfather, Baron Karl Pantzer, was stripped of the title in 1848 by King Wilhelm because of his association with the student's revolution against the state[48]. Karl made his escape to America and after four years' exile returned to Europe, taking refuge in Hungary. Later on, he was pardoned but his estates were confiscated. His family were left penniless and his eldest

---

[48] This information is from a newspaper report of an interview with Willie. However, King Wilhelm I reigned from 1861 which is inconsistent with the claim that Karl Pantzer was stripped of his title in 1848 (the year of the revolution). It may be that he was stripped of the title at a later time or that he was stripped of it by Wilhelm's predecessor (his brother, Frederick Wilhelm IV).

son, Charles [Willy's father], joined a circus, living a gypsy life, and eventually journeying to England, where he met his wife, Eliza Jones, who was a bareback rider in a hippodrome. Willy campaigned to have the Pantzer title and estate restored to the family and, in 1909, he was granted the title of Baron but, unfortunately, he failed in his bid to regain the estate and all its associated wealth.

Willy inherited his acrobatic skills from his parents and he established an act with his younger brother, Ernest, known not surprisingly as the *Pantzer Brothers*. Ernest was six years younger than Willy and he was twelve years old when he and Willy started performing together.

The brothers made their first appearance in England at the Royal Aquarium in London in December 1890 and they then undertook a short tour of the provinces appearing in Newcastle-upon-Tyne and Manchester, where they received good reviews.

I have not found any evidence of further performances in England until 1895 and it is possible that the brothers developed their act on continental Europe. They appeared in London in the summer of 1895 and then they went to America.

(Source: The herald. (Los Angeles [Calif.]), 15 March 1896. Chronicling America: Historic American Newspapers)

The brothers appeared at Proctor's Palace Theatre in New York where they were instant hits with the audiences. They remained in America for the next five years and they took up American citizenship in 1899. Willy and Ernest were granted naturalisation on the twenty-fourth day of February. The date of their arrival in America is unclear although the most likely date was September 1895. This date is consistent with the fact that he and his brother appeared in London in August 1895 and they appeared in New York in November of that year. However, their official naturalisation records state that they entered America on the tenth day of December 1893. No doubt, the date was chosen to fulfil the legal requirement that an individual had to be resident in America for five years before he could apply for naturalisation.

Willy and Ernest did not remain in America much longer and they returned to Europe in August 1899 to undertake a tour of Berlin, Paris and London. When they appeared at the London Hippodrome in 1900, their act was described as follows:

The Pantzer Brothers appear in ordinary morning dress only removing their coats when they warm with their work. They are not only very strong and expert head and hand balancers and equilibrists, but are also very funny fellows, introducing many little touches which send the delighted audience into roars of laughter. While one sustains the other "head to head", each plays an instrument of music. They also keep a large ball bouncing from pole to pole in time with the air they render on the mandolin and guitar.

It was about this time that Willy probably first considered the idea of introducing children and midgets into his act. Ernest was now twenty-one years old and no doubt the brothers were finding their balancing act more difficult to perform. Willy's first recruit was a diminutive boy who had been added to the act when they appeared in Hull in March 1902. He was probably Abe Pantzer, who was born William Archibald Cochran in Newcastle-upon-Tyne in 1895, the son of Archibald and Frances Cochran.

Lalla and Willy

It is unclear where Lalla and Willy met. It may have been in England in 1900 when the Pantzers began touring the country or it may have been the following year when both the Pantzers and the Selbinis were touring mainland Europe. Willy was a handsome man with a good physique. He boasted that he had a forty-inch chest that expanded to forty-four inches and his biceps were sixteen inches round. Given Lalla's natural beauty, she and Willy were obviously physically attracted to each other although their marriage was not to last. Willy and Lalla honeymooned in Nuremburg, Germany, where they performed at the Apollo Theatre in order to earn some money to help pay their bills.

Lalla gave birth to a daughter, Patricia Lalla Pantzer, on the twenty-eighth day of December 1902. According to the 1911 census, Patricia was born in London but I have failed to find any records of her birth. Lalla was eager to continue her show business career and I believe that Patricia was left in the care of her grandparents, Jack and Lily Selbini [McCoy].

Lalla had now developed a solo performance based on her act with the Selbini Troupe and Willy continued to perform with the Pantzer Brothers. For the next three years, they appeared on the same bill at venues across Europe although they continued to perform separate acts. They toured England, Germany, France, Belgium, and Russia, each act receiving good reviews wherever they appeared. It was possibly during this period that Willy taught the tsar of Russia, Nicholas II, how to box. Willy recounted the story sometime later and it was reported in *The Los Angeles Herald* on the tenth day of February 1910:

But one man ever struck the tsar of Russia and lived. That man is Willy Pantzer, one of the performers at the Orpheum. It came about in this manner: Pantzer was playing in St Petersburg. The tsar had been ill and some method of restoring his health was sought. Some brilliant member of the royal suite thought boxing would be just the right thing. Pantzer, who is an expert with the gloves, was called in. Each day for six weeks he smote the royal cheek with padded mitts and threw the royal person all over the place. The tsar got strong and was pleased. Then Pantzer was offered the place of official muscle-maker for the royal household and the entire army. The contract looked too big for Pantzer so he gracefully but firmly declined and beat a hasty retreat to Paris. Another potent reason which prompted the refusal is given by Pantzer thus: "Favourites of the tsar cause jealousy among the royal suite. Some day the favourite is missing. In other words, he is put out of the way. I am rather fond of life, and I have yet to see my thirty-fifth birthday".

Willy and his brother Ernest applied for British Nationalisation in 1903 which was duly granted on the thirtieth day of June. They did not meet the condition of residence for five years prior to the application but they may have been granted citizenship because their mother was British. Willy signed the oath of allegiance as "Frederick William Pantzer". He retained his American citizenship and he held an American passport which was to be of considerable help to him during the First World War.

The Pantzer Brothers and Lalla embarked on a tour of South Africa in February 1904 where Willy "adopted" another son[49]. He was Harry Pantzer, a midget, who was born Adolf Kotze in Cape Colony, South Africa. His date of birth is not known but Willy always stated that he was older than Abe. When Willy and Lalla brought him back from their South African tour in 1904, the passenger list for their voyage to England stated that Harry was over twelve years old.

On their return from South Africa, Willy and Lalla joined the Moss tour of Great Britain, performing in Edinburgh and London. They then appeared in Dresden before returning to England to undertake further engagements and Harry joined Lalla to provide a comic element into her act[50]. When Lalla appeared in Hull in July 1905, the local newspaper reported:

There were many last night who appreciated Lalla Selbini in what was described as a cycling exhibition. It was not, however, only the bicycle tricks which won the applause, for she is an expert juggler, and her popularity was partly, no doubt, due to her droll little coloured attendant who performed some amusing antics.

Lalla became a big hit with the British public, especially the male members of the audiences and she received numerous fan letters. In an interview in 1905, she said that for one line of "love" she received, she got four pages of "food". On

---

[49] Willy treated all the boys in his troupe as his sons and provided them with homes and education but I suspect that his main motive was to create his troupe of acrobats rather than to create a family. He adopted boys from across the world so it may be that some of them were informally adopted while others were legally adopted, depending upon their country of origin. In interviews, Willy talked of retiring with his boys.

[50] Harry may also have performed with Willy at the same time.

average, she received nightly three invitations to supper. She quoted two examples of her fan mail:

'My Dear Little Girl, I think you look perfectly sweet on your bicycle; I have quite fallen in love with you. I want you to come to supper with me. You need not be at all afraid to come, as I am 80 years old. If you consent to come, wear the enclosed red ribbon round your pretty neck.'

And in a more orthodox style:

'Dear Miss Selbini, I have been every night this week to see you. Your face haunts me. I feel I love you. I do so want to see you off the stage. Do you look as young off as on? The make-up is so deceptive. Will you give the stage door keeper a message, making an appointment? I have a lovely tandem bicycle, and we might have a ride together, and get to know one another better. Yours, most devotedly.'

Lalla in 1904
(Image courtesy of *"prints-4-all"*)

In December 1903, Ernest Pantzer announced that he had signed a new contract with his brother Willy for four more years and that the report, that he was going to do an act with his wife, was not founded on fact. However, the brothers did part company in 1905 and Ernest went on to perform with his own troupe of acrobats. Perhaps the brothers felt that their act could be taken no further. Ernest followed Willy's example by employing midgets in his act. He eventually returned to America but died of an aneurism in Phoenix, Arizona on the fourth day of March 1916 at the age of thirty-seven years.

Lalla Arrives in America

When Willy and Ernest separated, Lalla and Willy were about to embark on an engagement in America. The impresario Oscar Hammerstein I[51] had seen Lalla perform at the Rembrandt Theatre in Amsterdam in 1903 and he was impressed by her act and her beauty. In an article in the New York *Sun* newspaper in 1919, it stated that he:

"first saw Selbini when as a child in her early teens she made her debut at the Rembrandt Theatre in Holland. A year later found the little cyclist already established as the toast of Paris because of her perfect figure and lovely smile".

The article is basically correct except that Lalla was twenty-five years old! She did not perform as a solo artist until after 1900 and she started touring after she had married Willy Pantzer in 1902. Hammerstein gave her a contract to go to America, where she appeared at Hammerstein's Roof Garden.

Willy, Abe, and Harry accompanied Lalla to America, although I do not believe that Willy had secured any engagements for his troupe at the time. Harry, of course, was fundamental to Lalla's act. A third acrobat named Frederick Sylvester, aged nineteen years, also accompanied them. He was possibly a black servant that Willy employed to look after his boys.

Lalla's debut in America was preceded by publicity which claimed that she was French and she was billed as "La belle baigneuse" – the bathing beauty. The focus was clearly on her

---

[51] Oscar Hammerstein I was the father of Oscar Hammerstein II, who was half of the famous musical writers, Rodgers and Hammerstein.

beauty rather than on her cycling and juggling skills and her act was modified to take advantage of her physical attributes. The *New York Evening Telegram* reported on the eleventh day of May 1906, prior to Lalla's arrival in New York:

The first of the European acts to be announced for Hammerstein's Paradise Roof Garden is Mlle Lalla Selbini ("La Belle Baigneuse"). Mlle Selbini is a Parisian who has been the rage of the Paris music halls during last season on account of her face and physique. Mlle Selbini has won a number of medals from various photographic salons, having posed for a dozen or more prize winning photographs. She will appear at Hammerstein's Roof Garden in a bicycle act. She has won the title "La Belle Baigneuse" from the fact that the costume worn during her speciality is a bathing suit.

Hammerstein's Roof Garden, Broadway
(Source: Wikimedia Commons [public domain])

144

Lalla went along with the pretext that she was French, even to the point of putting on a fake French accent when she was interviewed by Alice Rohe of the New York newspaper, the *Evening World:*

Mlle Selbini can drop into a most delightful French accent just to please a newspaper writer looking for local colour. As a matter of fact, Lalla Selbini is Spanish, born in Madrid[52], but she has lived in London and Paris so long that she speaks English with a slight Parisian accent. Furthermore, all her mannerisms are French, as is her vaudeville act – decidedly so.

Alice Rohe was a pioneering American journalist and photographer who had her own column in the *Evening World* newspaper called "The Girl from Kansas" which ran regularly on page three. She wrote two articles about Lalla in early June 1906. In the first article, Lalla admitted that her cheeks were always "pretty pink and white" because she had a tattooed complexion. In the second article, she attributed her beauty to "avoiding corsets, late suppers, liquor, and inaction" and to taking three cold baths a day. There is no mention in either article of her private life.

When Lalla started performing in New York, her act caused a sensation but she received mixed reviews. Sime Silverman, the founder and editor of *Variety* magazine wrote in his review on the ninth day of June 1906:

Formerly a member of the Selbini Family of bicycle riders, Lalla Selbini, one of the daughters, appears on Hammerstein's

---

[52] The newspaper report was the only time that it was mentioned that Lalla was Spanish. Of course, she was British, being born on the Isle of Man.

Roof Garden this week for the first time in this country in a single act. It isn't so much what the young woman does as what she wears that will attract attention. Well made up, looking almost handsome on the stage, Miss Selbini after a few simple juggling tricks discards her costume, appearing as nature intended her with only a skin-tight piece of cloth separating her natural colour from the gaze of the audience. Without the aid of corsets she presents a figure that excites admiration, and while riding a wheel assumes positions that leave little to the imagination. The tricks performed are familiar and not difficult. A boy in black face acts as comedy assistant, but there are no laughs, only gasps. Miss Selbini is frankly indecent in her exhibition and will probably be talked about, becoming a drawing card thereby. As a "living picture" she is immense.

The *New York Dramatic Mirror* was more complimentary:

This was the first appearance in America of Lalla Selbini, known as "La Belle Baigneuse" from the fact that she appears during her act as a bather, wearing a tight-fitting bathing suit that displays her figure to perfection. Mlle. Selbini is a very beautiful woman and would attract attention anywhere on that account. She is also an accomplished bicyclist and juggler, and performed a number of diverting tricks in an engaging way. She is assisted by a small comedian, who appears in black-face.

Humorous Illustration of Lalla's Act

(Image courtesy of California Digital Newspaper Collection, Centre for
Bibliographic Studies and Research, University of California, Riverside,
http://cdnc.ucr.edu)

The old adage in the entertainment world that "there is no
such thing as bad publicity" was certainly true for Lalla. She
became a sensation and appeared at Hammerstein's Roof
Garden every night for the next sixteen weeks. No doubt, the
public were keen to see what the fuss was about! A further
review by Variety magazine on the fourteenth day of July
simply fanned the flames and created more public interest:

*The exposé of her outward femininity is still continued by
Lalla Selbini, "the bathing beauty". Miss Selbini may be of
the opinion that her costume is decorous to a degree. It might
be on a South Sea Island where all covering is scorned, but*

147

her appearance on the stage draws several gasps of astonishment and the title of "Lalla" is voted quite apropos.

Hammerstein was so enchanted by Lalla's beauty that when he built the Manhattan Opera House in 1906, he decorated it with her portraits. In a studio especially erected for the purpose, she posed every day between afternoon and evening performances for the paintings. Since that time, it is claimed, many artists in the world craved for the privilege of painting her.

Some members of the public were so outraged by Lalla's act that they complained to the authorities, resulting in Lalla being arrested. *The Pittsburgh Press* reported on the twenty-third day of September 1906:

When Mile. Lalla Selbini made her debut as a vaudeville star at the Hammerstein Roof Garden in New York, she created a genuine sensation. Her act, "The Bathing Girl," had been extensively exploited by a staff of energetic press agents and all New York was anxious to get a glimpse of the pretty woman who dared appear on the stage garbed in regulation bathing costume. On the opening night, when Miss Selbini stepped before the footlights, the audience sat dumbfounded for a second or two, then there ensued the wildest sort of a scene. Selbini was there with the bathing suit, all right, and it was one of the sort concerning which humorists are wont to speak. The next day the papers described that bathing costume and Selbini's fame was firmly established. Some of the critics made bold to assert that Selbini's remarkable beauty, so much of which was in evidence, made it possible for her to go a few steps further than any other actress had ever attempted. Then there was trouble. Several women who had witnessed the performance complained to the authorities and Miss Selbini was arrested. Speaking of the matter in a letter to Resident Manager Orr, of the Gayety, where Miss Selbini is to appear this week, she says: "It Is true that I was arrested, some of the prudes seeming to think the bathing costume in which I appear in my act was a trifle too scant. When I was given the opportunity to face these women I asked them if they had never appeared in bathing costume at public bathing places where thousands were assembled and every one of them admitted that she had. I then asked them to describe their water costumes and they did so, when it came out that I had enough material in my bathing garment to make two of some of those wore by my critics. To make a long story short the action against me was dropped".

Lalla clearly felt that her act was artistic rather than vulgar. She wrote an article which appeared in a number of publications:

THE IMMODESTY OF THE PEEK-A-BOO WAIST[53]

by Lalla Selbini, French Actress

It is far easier to make a definition of immodesty than of modesty. Immodesty can be typified by two words, in my estimation – the "peek-a-boo waist".

While I appear every afternoon and evening on the roof garden in a tight-fitting bathing suit, I must confess my sense

---

[53] The "peek-a-boo waist" was a fashionable garment in the early twentieth century. It was a blouse made from sheer fabric, which led to complaints that flesh could be seen through the eyelets in the embroidery or through the thin fabric.

of modesty would never go as far as to wear a peek-a-boo waist.

There is nothing more immodest than one of these suggestive, half-revealing, half-concealing garments that women have taken as a part of their costuming.

Someone has said that for me to criticise peek-a-boo waists is a little strange, since my appearance is so utterly unhampered by conventional clothing. Let me make one point clear; there is nothing more immodest about a woman's figure in a tight-fitting bathing suit than in a statue. While a woman may appear on the stage in a costume which accentuates an act she is giving, it is a part of her stage-profession. So long as it is not vulgar from an aesthetic sense, it cannot be vulgar at all. Real vulgarity or immodesty can only exist where the artistic sense is shocked, and to a pure mind with artistic instincts dominating it, there cannot be susceptibility to immodest suggestions.

The Venus of Medici is an exquisite figure. I am sure there are few people who would admit being shocked at this old Greek statue. Yet, how infinitively vulgar and suggestive she would be if some shocked lady would garb her in a peek-a-boo waist.

On the street, I think women should wear street clothes. The peek-a-boo waist with its multitudinous holes, its glimpse of lingerie and coloured ribbons is far more immodest than the so-called outrageously low-necked gown of the English society woman or the strip tights of the beautifully formed actress.

American women have gained a reputation of discretion as compared to the French women, but I must say that we would never be guilty of going the lengths of displaying our persons as the apparently conventional American women do in the peek-a-boo waist.

The "Dainty Duchess" Burlesque Company

While Lalla was performing at the Roof Garden, Willy was planning their next step. Unknown to her, he negotiated a contract for himself and Lalla with Weber and Rush to appear with their *Dainty Duchess Burlesque Company*, each with their own act. Willy claimed that he had sought the contract to avoid being separated from Lalla which would have been the case if she undertook a vaudeville tour. And, of course, it was an opportunity for Willy to further his own career. Keen to secure Lalla's services, Weber and Rush signed a contract with Willy without seeing his performance, prepared to risk that he may be a failure. *Variety* magazine reported on the twenty-first day of July 1906:

WEBER & RUSH HAVE SELBINI
"The Bathing Beauty", Lalla Selbini, now appearing au naturel on Hammerstein's roof, will travel next season with Weber & Rush's "Dainty Duchess" burlesque company as the feature[54]. Willie Pantzer, of the Pantzer Brothers, with a new act will also be a number in the same show, the two having been booked together. Miss Selbini made a statement that she had signed no contract with Weber and Rush and did not know whether she would go under their management, but as her husband signed the contract for her appearance the firm is satisfied that Miss Selbini will appear.

Weber and Rush clearly saw Lalla as the major attraction in their show and they planned to build upon the reputation that she had gained while performing at Hammerstein's Roof

---

[54] The "feature" was the top-billed act; the major advertised attraction.

Garden. They organised advanced publicity in the towns where the company was scheduled to play:

When "the bathing girl", Lalla Selbini, starts on the road with Weber & Rush's "Dainty Duchess" burlesque company there will precede her along the route of the show a row of three sheets having a photograph taken of herself "as iz" in highly coloured designs. Following the billposters will be another brigade to keep the natives away from the fence. Nothing like Selbini's pictures have been shown in the wilds and Anthony Comstocks[55] are expected to spring up galore. That contingency will be catered for however, and the posters will be draped wherever and whenever possible.

The star billing was enough to appease Lalla and she added her signature to the contract that Willy had negotiated with Weber and Rush and the "Dainty Duchess" company opened their season at the Harlem Music Hall on the twenty-fifth day of August 1906. The press soon recognised that Willy and Lalla were the strongest acts in the "Dainty Duchess" show and they were instant hits with the audiences. A review of the opening night of the show stated:

Lalla Selbini and the Willy Pantzer Troupe are the two strongest items in the olio. Miss Selbini with her candid display of her charming contours does the sort of act burlesque audiences like to watch and Willy Pantzer has an acrobatic act of exceptional merit.

Any concerns that Weber and Rush may have had about Willy's act were unfounded. *Variety* reported in September:

[55] Anthony Comstock (1844-1915) was a United States Postal Inspector and politician dedicated to ideals of Victorian morality.

Weber & Rush signed Willie Pantzer for their "Dainty Duchess" show before Mr Pantzer gave a trial performance of the acrobatic act he now presents. His success has caused the firm to feel elated over their foresight.

Willy's new act involved him in developing the acrobatic and comic performance he had perfected with his brother but he now used his adopted sons to support him. He recognised that he could perform more spectacular acrobatics by using small children and midgets which were not possible if he had used adults.

Lalla's doubts regarding the contract soon began to surface again. She had started up a friendship with the illusionist, The Great Lafayette, who was touring America at the time. She sought his advice on the contract and he put doubts in her mind, suggesting that she could get better terms than those that Willy had got for her. It was rumoured that Lafayette had even asked Lalla to join his company. Consequently, Lalla sought to cancel the contract, although there was no likelihood that she would be able to do so.

Willy was incensed about the situation and he put the blame firmly on Lafayette. He suspected Lalla and Lafayette of "having feelings" for each other although he never publically accused them of having an affair. It was alleged that he accused Lafayette of alienating Lalla's affections and he allegedly sued him for damages. In reply, Lafayette wrote Willy a "scorching" letter, calling him sundry uncomplimentary names for misrepresenting *"the most beautiful and virtuous woman in the world"*. The letter read so well, from a legal point of view, it was reported, that it was the opinion of those who saw it that it was written by Lafayette's attorney. The alleged lawsuit was reported in the *New York Herald* on the sixth day of September 1906:

ACROBAT SUES MAGICIAN
William Pantzer Demands $50,000 off "Lafayette" for Alleged Alienation of Wife's Affection.

William Pantzer, a vaudeville acrobat, has brought a suit against an illusionist in the same business. Known as "Lafayette", [Willy is] asking $50,000 damages, alleging the alienation of the affections of Mrs Pantzer, who under the name of Lalla Selbini does a bicycle act in vaudeville houses. Mrs Pantzer has been performing at Hammerstein's Victoria and it is alleged that when Pantzer announced to his wife that he had arranged for her participation in a show in which he was to be the principal[56], she told him that she had made an engagement for a principal part in Lafayette's show. Hence, the suit.

No doubt, it was Willy's actions regarding the contract that had turned Lalla against him. Lafayette clearly made matters worse. There were no further reports on the lawsuit so it is unclear whether it proceeded or not. Indeed, Willy denied that he had brought the suit. However, Willy and Lalla were contractually obliged to fulfil the engagement with Weber and Rush and there was an uneasy truce between Lalla and Willy. Their separate acts continued to be crowd pleasers and Weber and Rush were keen to retain their services but Lalla made life

---

[56] There is no doubt that Lalla was to be the principal attraction of the show so Willy was deluding himself by claiming he was to be the star [unless the newspaper misquoted him].

difficult. She reported sick on occasions and when the show performed in Ohio in December 1906, Lalla took offence over the fact that a local girl who was in the show was featured in the local press and she had been "ignored". *Variety* magazine reported the incident:

TROUBLE IN THE "DAINTY DUCHESS"

After effects in the Weber & Rush's "Dainty Duchess" burlesque company will probably result from the recent disagreement at Youngstown, Ohio, between Lalla Selbini and Gladys Carlyle. Miss Selbini is the "feature" of the show, while Miss Carlyle was "principal boy". In the Ohio town, Miss Carlyle's birthplace, the papers saw her first and most often. Miss Selbini threatened to leave the show if someone did not keep better control over the newspaper men. This was smoothed over, at the cost to Miss Carlyle of her position with the troupe, her release becoming necessary to appease the "feature". Now Miss Selbini avows she will leave the "Dainty Duchess" anyway before the show plays in Boston, which will be in three weeks. "The Bathing Beauty" claims to hold a telegram from Weber & Rush saying "Will release week before Boston". The firm says if such a wire is in existence, it is a forgery. Ed F Rush was in Buffalo this week, where the company is playing, and may have accomplished an amicable settlement of the controversy, caused it is claimed through Miss Selbini believing she and her husband (Will Pantzer, who travels in the same organisation, having an acrobatic act of his own, distinct from his wife) have a larger earning capacity in vaudeville than their present salary returns them. It has been a matter of some difficulty to handle Miss Selbini since the "Duchess" opened at the beginning of the season, but Weber & Rush make the positive statement that the pair will either play out their contract or cease working professionally on this side [of the Atlantic] until they do.

Of course, Willy supported Lalla to protect his own position. Being men of business, Weber and Rush recognised the pulling power of both acts and they tried to find a solution which was agreeable to all parties. Gladys Carlyle transferred to their sister company "The Bon Tons" and they tried to negotiate a new contract with Willy and Lalla. *Variety magazine* reported on the fourteenth day of December 1906:

During the recent visit in Chicago of Ed F. Rush, of Weber and Rush, it developed that the firm seriously contemplates starring Willy Pantzer and Lalla Selbini (his wife), both at present with "Dainty Duchess" company, in a musical play next season. Mr. Rush was reticent and no details were given out by him concerning it.

However, the proposal never came to fruition. A report in *Variety* on the twelfth day of January 1907 claimed that Weber and Rush had agreed that Lalla would leave the show in two weeks' time and that Willy would remain on the show although the claim was subsequently proven to be incorrect. They did agree, however, to let Lalla take time out from the show to appear at Hammerstein's Roof Garden for the week beginning the eleventh day of February 1907. Perhaps they felt that she needed time to cool down!

Lalla's appearances with the "Dainty Duchess" company had become lacklustre and Weber and Rush made one final attempt to win her over by making her another proposal. They proposed that she should lead her own company under their management. It was also proposed by the firm that Willy should travel with the show, but he said that he preferred vaudeville as he did not relish the idea of having his identity smothered, no provision having been proposed for featuring him jointly with Lalla. Although she turned down the offer, it was clear that Lalla was considered the bigger star which Willy obviously resented and their relationship would no longer be the same.

Willy and Lalla continued to fulfil their contract, albeit reluctantly but Lalla's appearances with the show were becoming less frequent and she finally left in April 1907. *Variety* reported on the thirteenth day of April:

Lalla Selbini, "the Bathing Beauty", will close with the "Dainty Duchess" Company next week, leaving immediately for Europe[57]. Edith Booth, another member of the same show, will probably accompany her. Willy Pantzer, Miss Selbini's husband, will remain here to play Hammerstein's Roof this summer.

Willy and Lalla never appeared together on the same bill again. It was clear that their relationship was over. Willy played a few more dates with the "Dainty Duchess" company before leaving but the parting was acrimonious. He sued Weber and Rush in July 1907 for loss of earnings:

PANTZER SUING MANAGERS - A suit for $450 has been brought against Weber& Rush by Willy Pantzer for the amount of the last week's salary, he and his wife Lalla

---

[57] Although Lalla left the show, she did not leave for Europe but continued to perform in America for some time.

Selbini, were entitled to as the features of the "Dainty Duchess" show last season.

Weber and Rush claimed that Willy owed them money which is why they withheld the salary but they settled on a compromise one week before the case was due to be heard at the New York Municipal Court by paying Willy $200. Willy and Lalla had been separated over six months at the time of the settlement and the payment that Willy received was possibly equal to or greater than Willy's wage given the fact that he and Lalla had been contracted by Weber and Rush on the reputation of Lalla [although Willy may have negotiated a single fee for both of them]. Willy's act had been unseen at the time. Indeed, it had only had its first trial run in July 1906 without creating any great press interest.

Willy filed for divorce from Lalla in Michigan on the fourteenth day of December 1908 on the grounds of "extreme cruelty". The grounds were probably chosen to enable the divorce to go through quickly without needing to provide any evidence. Lalla did not contest the suit (she was not in America at the time) and a decree absolute was granted on the twentieth day of May 1909. Their daughter, Patricia, remained in the care of her grandparents, Jack and Lily Selbini [McCoy] in England.

Willy: Life After Lalla

Willy stayed in New York throughout 1907, appearing at a number of different theatres, including a summer season at Hammerstein's Roof Garden, where Lalla had made her debut. When Willy and Lalla separated, Harry, who had been supporting Lalla, joined Willy's troupe and Willy created his "acro-pantomimic" sketch called "The Limit" which was a big success in New York. The cast for the sketch also included Jewel Pantzer and Paul Pantzer [obviously, not their real names], in addition to Willy, Harry, and Abe. Jewel and Paul were recruited in America and they did not travel with Willy when he left America in 1910.

Willy toured America throughout 1908 and he then added a new interest in his life. In addition to managing his own affairs, he began managing a duo of female comedy singers, Lillian and Anna Doherty. The Doherty Sisters had been performing since about 1899 when in their early teens, and they had had a successful career, performing in both America and Europe. Willy billed them as *"The Famous Ginger Girls"*:

The Doherty Sisters, the famous "Ginger Girls",
Management Willy Pantzer
Overpowering animal spirits, wonderful clothes, preternatural nerve and good, fine, rollicking fun assist a pair of husky young women, who call themselves the Doherty Sisters, to captivate all of the audience they do not scare into a fit. They leap out with about all the clothes missing which cannot be spangled and hung from the shoulder blades. They wear pink fleshings [flesh coloured tights worn by actors]

under this diaphanous apology for array and are altogether breezy. Both are good-looking and have a line of chatter which would make Smith and Campbell[58] atop to think. They make quick and amusing changes, and one of them, handsome, babbling over with vitality and romp, has first-class low comedy talent in the raw, but a great deal noisier and better than Premier's[59].

The Doherty Sisters in 1910
(Image courtesy of California Digital Newspaper Collection, Centre for Bibliographic Studies and Research, University of California, Riverside, http://cdnc.ucr.edu)

Perhaps Willy's motives were not just professional as he started an affair with the younger sister, Anna! She was

[58] Smith and Campbell were a comedy duo who specialised in "sidewalk repartee".
[59] Probably a theatre in New York.

previously married to and divorced from William Connelly, known professionally as William Inman, a comedian. Willy and the Doherty Sisters appeared on the same bill at a number of venues throughout 1909 and 1910.

Willy had to cancel an engagement in February 1909 to defend an action brought against him for a breach of a contract he had signed in Germany some years before. I do not have any details of the suit; nor do I know its outcome although it may be the same breach of contract lawsuit that Lalla had problems with in Vienna (see later).

Following his divorce from Lalla, Willy and Anna married at St Paul in Minnesota on the twenty-seventh day of November 1909. In 1910 Willy and the Doherty Sisters set sail for engagements overseas. Willy applied for a passport in New York on the twenty-eighth day of June 1910 stating that he would be returning to America in about three months time. He and the Doherty Sisters left soon afterwards and they arrived in Southampton on the eighth day of July. They had a contract for a three month engagement at the Hippodrome Theatre in London, after which they planned to return to America. However, the Australian impresario, James Cassius Williamson, was passing through London at that time, on his way to an engagement on the Continent. He was aware of Willy's reputation and he took time out to see his act. He soon realised that the act was exactly what he wanted for his up and coming pantomime in Australia. It was reported that:

"before he [Mr Williamson] went to bed that night, the contracts had been drawn up and signed and everything was fixed for the Australian engagement".

While they were in Great Britain, Willy and Anna took time out to visit Glasgow[60]. There, they saw an underfed urchin tumbling in the streets. Willy saw in him not only a born acrobat but a natural shrewdness which was readily adaptable to comedy purposes. Willy "adopted" his third son, Joe Pantzer. Joe's real name was (probably) Alexander McLachlan and he had had a very poor upbringing. In an interview that Willy and Anna gave in Australia, Anna said:

The little chap [Joe], who always has a smile for one, is from Glasgow. We are not sure of his age as we could not learn it exactly from his mother, who was constantly intoxicated. Indeed, we could scarcely ascertain his proper name. When he was first found huddled up in a doorway with his mother, he was a pitiable object, and I was the last one who would ever have thought of trying to make an acrobat of him, but my husband saw possibilities. We consider he is quite seven years behind his normal growth, stunted by lack of nourishment and ordinary care. When he first came to us, he had never had a bath, never tasted soup, which, when given to him, made him ill, and did not know the uses of ordinary garments.

Willy and his troupe and the Doherty Sisters left for Australia on the twenty-eighth of October 1910. There was no chance that Willy would return to America within three months!

Willy and the Doherty Sisters travelled on board the *SS Majestic* from New York to Southampton and the passenger list for the arrivals included the following entries:

---

[60] I have not found any evidence that Willy performed in Glasgow at the time so it is not obvious why he would go there. Perhaps, he simply wanted a break from performing.

- Wm Pantzer, single male (or not accompanied by his wife), American
- Leila Pantzer, single female (or not accompanied by her husband), American
- Alice Pantzer, single female (or not accompanied by her husband), American

These records are almost certainly for Willy and the Doherty Sisters although they contain a number of errors. Leila and Alice are probably Lillian and Anna Doherty. They and Willy travelled first class which is why no profession is recorded for them (professions were only recorded for second and third class passengers).

In Australia, Willy and his troupe and the Doherty Sisters performed their speciality acts in the pantomime "Jack and the beanstalk" which toured for twelve months. Both acts were well received. However, the Doherty Sisters announced that they would separate at the end of the tour and Anna planned to go solo.

While on tour, Willy added a fourth son to his troupe. He adopted Thomas Burke, the six year old son of Edward and Sarah Burke from Hobart. A letter from the British Foreign Office to Thomas in 1954 confirmed his date of adoption as the twenty-fifth day of September 1911 and that his adoptive parents were *Charles William and Lalla Pantzer*. However, the original deeds could not be located and it would appear that the adoptive parents names were wrongly reported; they should have been Frederick (or Heinrich) William and Anna Pantzer.

After Willy completed his tour of Australia, he had planned a busy schedule to undertake engagements in South Africa,

England, Paris, Germany, and America, and he then planned to return to Australia in 1913. But, to quote Robert Burns, "the best laid schemes of mice and men often go awry" and circumstances were to radically change Willy's plans.

Initially, all went to plan. He and Anna toured South Africa for ten weeks, they undertook engagements in England, and then they appeared at the Folies Bergère in Paris. When in Paris, Willy was taken ill and he had to cancel a planned appearance at the Wintergarten in Berlin. He then returned to England to undertake further engagements but, in August 1913, it was reported that Anna was to sue Willy for divorce on the grounds of adultery, naming a "foreign woman of the stage" as correspondent. Anna filed for divorce in Michigan on the thirty-first day of October 1913 but the grounds were recorded as "extreme cruelty" since positive evidence would have been required to prove adultery. The decree absolute was granted on the twentieth day of February 1914.

Following the break up with Anna, Willy finally managed to fulfil his commitment to perform in Germany but he was back in England in the spring of 1914. He married again, for the third time, in London on the eighth day of March 1914. His bride was Hortense Ida Helene Koschke, who was twenty years younger than him[61]. Hortense was born in Ujvidek in Hungary in 1894. She may have been the person that Anna claimed Willy was unfaithful with.

---

[61] Hortense may have been known as Ida.

Hortense Ida Helene Koschke
(Courtesy of Ancestry.co.uk)

It was at this time that Harry, the Boer that Willy and Lalla brought back from South Africa in 1904, was charged with assaulting an eight year old girl. Willy argued in his defence that he was of previous good character and he [Willy] could not account for his [Harry's] behaviour. Willy also argued that Harry was a key part of his act which would be practically of no use without him. Harry was fortunate to escape with a fine.

After appearing at a few more theatres in England, Willy and his troupe travelled to Austria where they were booked to appear at the Apollo Theatre in Vienna at the beginning of August. The timing could not have been worse! Archduke Franz Ferdinand of Austria had been assassinated on the twenty-eighth day of June and Britain declared war on Germany on the fourth day of August. The Great War had begun and Willy and his troupe were in the middle of the action. Willy's brother, Ernest, had been in Europe at the same time but he managed to obtain passage from Brussels to London and then on to America. He reported that he had no news of Willy or his mother and sister who were also on the continent. Willy was not so lucky as his brother and he found himself and members of his troupe trapped in Austria for the duration of the war[62]. As an American citizen, he was able to obtain permits allowing him to travel about Europe but the Austrian authorities would not allow the British members of his troupe such freedom[63]. Indeed, Willy could possibly have obtained permission to travel to America but, to his credit, he would not abandon his "boys". He earned a living as best he could, but at the end of the war his application for a new passport to allow him to return to America illustrated how difficult times were. He stated that he wished to travel to the United States but he was unable to state when that would be as he did not have sufficient funds to pay the fares for his troupe members.

Hortense gave birth to a son, Alfred Harry William Pantzer, on the third day of February 1916 when they were in Vienna. However, the relationship between Willy and Hortense broke down and they started divorce proceedings in 1921 while still on the European continent. At that time, Willy was working in Rome, Hortense was living in Vienna, and the lawsuit was due to be heard in Berlin. It may be that the case never proceeded since they did not divorce until 1937 although there was apparently no lasting reconciliation. The costs and the

---

[62] The *New York Dramatic Mirror* reported incorrectly on May 20, 1916 that "Willie Pantzer had been killed while fighting with the German Army".
[63] Willy was also a naturalised British subject but it was obviously not wise to admit it.

logistics of travelling between the European cities probably proved too great.

Willy never returned to live in America. He remained on the continent for a while, fulfilling engagements and adding to his troupe. He made England his base and he became a star attraction in the theatres and circuses, being billed as *The World Renowned Willy Pantzer and His Wonderful Midgets*. He established a troupe of performers, usually ten or twelve in number, with at least half of them being midgets. He developed a show which consisted of three acts, the first one to demonstrate the troupe's acrobatic skills, the second one to demonstrate the troupe's musical and comedic skills, and the third one had two of his midgets performing a comedy boxing match. He kept this basic formula throughout his career, which continued up to 1948 when the troupe was disbanded. Willy's prime role was to manage the troupe and over time, he began to be less active in the performances. The troupe was in constant demand and they appeared in many British provincial theatres and abroad. They may have performed in the United States. In an interview that Willy gave to a reporter, Richard Parsons, at the time of his retirement, he spoke of being in the United States where *"distinguished people posed for pictures with the Great Little Men and one of the midgets [Charlie] challenged Jack Dempsey, world heavyweight boxing champion, to a spoof fight"*. However, I have not found any evidence in newspapers, such as articles or advertisements, to corroborate the story.

When Willy came to England, he brought his son Alfred with him but his wife, Hortense, remained on the continent. Little is known about her after this time but Willy filed for divorce (again) in 1937, naming two correspondents; Otto Kriesler and George Chevalier. Not that Willy had remained celibate during the period of separation from Hortense. He met Hilda Littler, also known as Hilda Bland, in the early 1920s, possibly when he was touring mainland Europe. Hilda was part of a show business family and she and Willy soon entered into a relationship. Hilda travelled with the troupe on tour but it is unclear whether she performed with them or not.

Willy and his family, including the members of his troupe, lived at Pantzer Mansions in Brighton. In 1932, Hilda formerly changed her name to Hilda Pantzer and, in 1933, Willy was granted British citizenship[64]. After his divorce from Hortense, Willy and Hilda married in Brighton in 1940. Willy died on the twenty-eighth day of May 1955 at the Royal Sussex County Hospital in his eighty-third year, although his death record gives his age as seventy-six years. His estate was valued at over four thousand pounds.

---

[64] Willy had previously been granted UK naturalisation in 1903 under the name of Frederick William Pantzer but it may have become invalidated for some reason. Perhaps, because Willy was born in Germany, he had to re-apply after the end of the First World War.

Lalla Goes It Alone in America

Although the newspapers reported that Lalla was to travel to Europe immediately after she left the "Dainty Duchess" company, this was not the case. She remained in America where she went on tour with the Orpheum circuit of vaudeville shows, founded by Martin Beck, for the next year in an attempt to rebuild her career without Willy. She continued with her familiar act of trick cycling, supported by a black-faced midget who provided the comedy. Her career began to flourish again and when she appeared at the Gaiety Theatre in Washington in January 1908, she was billed as the highest salaried burlesque artiste. Lalla still exploited her natural beauty by wearing her "sensational" costumes. However, with some of her engagements, she chose to wear "more respectable" clothes to appease the authorities.

Harry Pantzer had originally supported Lalla but he remained with Willy's troupe and Lalla recruited a replacement. A report in *Variety Magazine* in September 1909 referred to the midget as "Lalla's little brother Ching Ching" but, of course, he was not related to Lalla. I have not established his real name but he used the stage name *Archie Selbini*.

Lalla appeared in Chicago, Philadelphia, San Francisco, New Orleans, Kansas City, and Indianapolis, where she was well-received by audiences and she received favourable reviews for her act. For example:

San Francisco: Standing upon an inverted bicycle, a young woman of seemingly angular physique doffs her loose gown and reveals a Juno-like figure in a blue and white bathing costume that clings to her curves. This act of self-

transformation is the most stunning – not to say agreeable – surprise of the few afforded by the Orpheum's current programme. She is billed as "Lalla Selbini, the bathing beauty" but all the bathing she does is in the calcium rays. Her garb is better adapted to emphasize her perfection of form than would ordinary tights, trunks and blouse. But if she does not go in swimming, Miss Selbini does several other things that prove her entitled to headline honours even if she were less shapely. She juggles and rides bicycles and unicycles, in all of which she is comically aided by a diminutive boy in Chinese apparel, who is no mean acrobat, and an educated fox terrier. Another surprising effect of the performance is its development from mediocrity to a rousing finale.

Philadelphia: The most beautiful woman on the stage today is Mlle. Lalla Selbini, who appears in her own creation which she titled "The Parisian Bathing Girl." Mlle. Selbini is equally at home as a singer, dancer, trick cycle rider and gymnast, and her act is one of the most pleasing in all the range of the varieties.

Lalla completed her tour of America by appearing at a number of theatres in New York but the critics there were less complimentary. She appeared again at Hammerstein's Roof Garden where she had caused a sensation eighteen months earlier and *Variety* commented:

Lalla Selbini, "the bathing beauty", is back with her offering slightly changed since her first appearing atop of the Victoria. She still retains the services of the midget, and with good judgment, for the diminutive one deserves the credit for the warm reception accorded. Miss Selbini has taken on considerable weight touring the country and her appearance in the bathing costume might be treated with a little discretion.

They were equally uncomplimentary when she appeared at Keith and Proctor's Pleasure Palace on Fifty-Eighth Street a few weeks' later:

Lalla Selbini dressed in character, sings "Mariutch Down at Coney Isle" while her midget assistant, in a burlesque dressing of a dancer, cavorts about the stage. The midget is much the greater part of the number. Miss Selbini appearance in the unlovely garb of an Italian following her appearance as "the bathing beauty" left a disagreeable impression, for which the fun of the song was no compensation.

Lalla's problems mounted up while she was in New York. She signed a contract to appear for a month at De Coste's theatres in Cuba on the understanding that De Coste would provide transportation for her and her midget. When such transportation failed to arrive, she sued De Coste for breach of contract. The case became very complex. Lalla had agreed the contract with De Coste's agent in New York, one Fermien Ruiz. However, De Coste denied that Ruiz had any authority to act as his agent and he [Ruiz] was awaiting trial in Havana for fraud. It transpired that Riuz had been embezzling the money that De Coste had provided for the cost of the transportation. Lalla was not the only artiste that Luiz had defrauded. Unfortunately for Lalla and the other acts, De Coste was not liable for the breach of contract and she did not

172

receive any compensation. She also had to pay her own costs of the legal action.

When Lalla thought that things could not get any worse in New York, she was accused of employing an underage child performer. The story was published in *Variety* on the sixteenth day of May 1908:

The Gerry Society[65] claims the midget employed by Lalla Selbini "the Bathing Girl" in her vaudeville act is under the prescribed age limit for stage children. Miss Selbini denies the claim and it will be thrashed out in the courts. On Monday night, at the Folly, Brooklyn, where Miss Selbini is playing this week, one of the Gerry agents turned up causing the midget and herself to appear before a magistrate. Bail was given, and the trial set down for next week. William Grossman, of House, Grossman, and Vorbaus, will appear for the defendants.

The Gerry Society was the common name of the New York Society for the Prevention of Cruelty to Children who, at that time, had excessive powers to intervene when they believed that a child was endangered. They had a particular dislike for the vaudeville stage which they considered was immoral and would corrupt minors. They caused such controversy with those involved in the theatre that an "anti-Gerry" campaign groups formed, and the mayor of New York was persuaded to limit Gerry's power and set out proper regulation of child stage performers.

---

[65] The Gerry Society was the same organisation that prevented Lalla's father, Jack Selbini, from performing with his children in New York in 1888.

173

The outcome of their accusation against Lalla is not known but, in the circumstances, it turned out to be irrelevant. Lalla had left New York and America and she set sail for England on board the *SS Majestic* on the twenty-seventh day of May 1908. Archie Selbini, the alleged under-age performer, accompanied her.

In spite of the poor press that she had received in New York, Lalla agreed a contract to return to America the following year with the Orpheum circuit. Variety magazine reported in August 1908 that the bill for the Orpheum road show for the following season was complete and that:

"Miss Selbini will return with two midgets and two girls, presenting an entirely new offering from the Bathing Girl [act] formerly shown by her".

Lalla Returns to Europe

Lalla arrived in Southampton on the fourth day of June 1908 and, after a two week engagement at the Coliseum Theatre in London, she undertook a tour of Continental Europe. She remained a star attraction and, according to *Variety Magazine*, she was earning $350 a week[66], more than she ever earned in America.

She started her continental tour at the Wintergarten in Germany, accompanied by her sister Mizpah. The *New York Clipper* commented:

The November programme is headed by Cleo De Merode but the real hit of the bill is Lalla Selbini, "the bathing beauty", that dainty little singer and phenomenal cycling expert, who charmed American playgoers to such an extent that her place has never been filled since her return to Europe.

Lalla then appeared at Steiner's English Garden in Vienna and she was a big success. However, while she was in Vienna, her past dealings caught up with her. A policeman entered her hotel room at seven o'clock in the morning and confiscated her clothes, money and jewellery due to her failure to fulfil an earlier contract. Lalla was later able to buy back her property. She claimed that she was forced to renege on the contract because she had to stay with her husband, Willy Pantzer, in America. Of course, the real reason perhaps was that Lalla had a better offer from Oscar Hammerstein! The lawsuit may well be the same one that Willy was called on to defend in

---

[66] In 1908, $350 dollars was equivalent to just over £70 sterling which, at the time, was the average annual wage in England.

America in February 1909. A report from Paris in *Variety Magazine* stated:

The property is being held until Miss Selbini fulfils contracts on the Continent made before she first appeared in America. The contracts call for a low salary. She contracted to play with the Orpheum Road Show in America this season, but has been obliged to cancel until she is through over here [Paris].

After her unfortunate experience in Vienna, Lalla went on to appear at the Marigny Theatre in Paris and at the Wintergarten in Berlin. Ironically, Lalla was billed as an "American Girl" when she appeared in Berlin whereas she was billed as a Parisian when she first appeared in New York!

Now without the prospect of the American tour, Lalla returned to engagements in England in early 1909. She was booked to appear at the Empire Theatre in London for eight weeks at a fee of £35 per week[67]. However, this booking was to cause more trouble for Lalla with broken contracts. When she was in Paris, she signed an agreement with the international theatrical agency, Marinelli and Co. Like all agencies, Marinelli arranged bookings for their artistes in return for a commission. They claimed that Lalla had failed to pay commission on a booking that they had arranged for Lalla to appear at the Empire Theatre but Lalla's defence was that her mother had arranged the booking and that she had been coerced into signing the agreement with Marinelli. The case was heard at the Westminster County Court and it was reported in many newspapers throughout the world. Perhaps

---

[67] This fee, although substantial, is half of that reported a year earlier in *Variety Magazine*.

the most complete report was the one published in the New Zealand newspaper, the *Otago Witness*, on the twelfth day of May, 1909:

A claim by Messrs Marinelli and Co, theatrical agents, against Miss Lalla Selbini, a member of the Selbini family of music hall performers, for £23 commission on performances at the Empire Theatre, Leicester Square, London, was heard in Westminster County Court. The plaintiff's case was that Miss Selbini signed an agreement to pay them commission on all engagements within a certain period. The defence was that Miss Selbini's mother obtained the Empire Theatre engagement. Miss Selbini, giving evidence, said she saw Mr Marinelli in Paris while performing there, and refused to sign an agreement with him. She was going on to Berlin, and Mr Marinelli told her she would find harder treatment there than she found in Vienna, because she would be met by men who would take the clothes off her back in the street unless she signed the contract with him. She signed under coercion. Explaining the reference to Vienna, the witness said the men burst into her room at 7 a.m. while she was in bed and carried off her clothing and jewellery because she had failed to carry out an old contract to perform in that city. Mr Marinelli, in evidence, gave a different version of the Paris interview. He told Miss Selbini she had broken four contracts in various cities, for which judgment had been entered against her, and that he could not act for her in Berlin unless she made him her sole agent. The Dresden Selbini contract was put in, in evidence. Deputy Judge Bevan (reading): "Miss Lalla Selbini, the Bathing Beauty". Mr Cranstoun (for defendant) said that was one of her performances. Was it likely that this young

*lady was a superior power in bargaining with Mr Marinelli?
The Deputy-judge: "If you ask me, I think she could twist him
round his little finger. When she turned her black eyes on me,
I was fascinated; my pen dropped from my fingers"(laughter).
Mr Cranstoun: "That is flattery". Judgment was given for
Messrs Marinelli and Co, with costs.*

The comment from the deputy judge seems hardly appropriate
although it probably did not affect the judgment. There was
little doubt that Lalla had signed the contract because it was in
her interest to do so and, legally, she was obliged to fulfil it.
One report stated that Lalla may appeal against the judgment
and the judge's comment may have provided suitable grounds
for such an appeal. However, there is no evidence that an
appeal was lodged.

Lalla appeared as the star attraction at a number of provincial
theatres throughout England in the early part of 1909 and then
she returned to Paris for a season. Her act was basically the
same one that she developed after she married Willy Pantzer.
In Paris, her act was advertised as:

*"Lalla Selbini in a mixture of dance and bicycle tricks with
her little brother Ching-Ching"*

She continued performing in Paris throughout much of 1910
but her career was about to take a new direction when she
renewed her acquaintance with the illusionist, The Great
Lafayette.

Lalla and Lafayette

(Source: The Frankfort Roundabout. (Frankfort, Ky.), 07 Jan. 1905.
Chronicling America: Historic American Newspapers)

The Great Lafayette was born Sigmund Neuberger, a Jew, and supposedly in Munich on the twenty-fifth day of February 1871. He immigrated to America where he took up American citizenship[68]. He began appearing in vaudeville as a sharpshooter with a bow and arrow but he developed his magic act after seeing the Chinese magician Ching Ling Foo in 1898. He developed a number of illusions and he became expert in quick-change routines. He soon established himself as a star attraction and he was reputed to be the highest paid entertainer of his time, earning the equivalent of two to three million pounds sterling per year. He had few friends and he

---

[68] He claimed in the 1911 census that he was born in Los Angeles and, after his death his brother claimed that their parents were American.

dedicated his life to his favourite dog, which had been given to him by his friend Harry Houdini, and to his business.

"The lion's bride"
(Source: The Indianapolis journal. (Indianapolis [Ind.]), 17 Jan. 1904.
Chronicling America: Historic American Newspapers)

Lafayette's most famous magic illusion was the "The Lion's Bride" which he introduced early in his career and he continually developed and changed it over a period of ten years. The basic story of the illusion remained constant. A live lion roared and pranced about in a cage in which a distressed female was thrown, in the presence of her lover (played by Lafayette), to face the ferocious beast. The lion would rear on its hind legs as if to pounce on the woman and then suddenly, it would be revealed that it was Lafayette (again) in a lion's costume, who would rescue the maiden.

The illusion was not without difficulties and Lafayette was attacked by the lion on more than one occasion, sustaining a number of minor injuries. On other occasions, the lion would not co-operate and it would remain placid. Such an occasion occurred when Lafayette appeared at Morrison's Theatre in New York in 1906 and the manager of the theatre withheld some of Lafayette's fee as compensation, resulting in a lawsuit. Soon after this incident, Lafayette brought his show to Great Britain where it became immensely popular and he set up a permanent residence in London.

Lalla met Lafayette in 1906 at Hammerstein's Theatre in New York, where they were both appearing, and they soon became good friends; perhaps surprisingly, because Lafayette did not make friends easily. As previously stated, Lafayette was involved with the dispute with Willy Pantzer over the "Dainty Duchess" contract. Although it was reported that Lafayette had made an offer to Lalla to join his show, she continued with her solo act until 1910. On her return from Paris, Lalla undertook an engagement in Glasgow at the end of 1910 and this booking enabled her to renew her acquaintance with Lafayette who was appearing in Edinburgh. Lafayette was faced with an emergency and he called upon Lalla to take the part of the princess in "The Lion's Bride" illusion. She played the part so successfully that Lafayette finally persuaded her to join his company and to continue the role of the princess.

Was the relationship between Lalla and Lafayette more than just platonic? Some authors have suggested that they were lovers but others claim that Lafayette was incapable of showing any affection to another human and that the only true love in his life was his favourite dog, Beauty. Paul Daniels, the British magician who was a great admirer of Lafayette, believes that he was a larger-than-life Liberace-type character[69] and that he was almost certainly homosexual. At one time when riding with a theatre manager, Lafayette appeared depressed and he said "Do you know? I'd sooner die for the sake of my horse than for any woman born". The theatre manager thought maybe that Lafayette had been jilted. On the evidence, it seems unlikely that Lalla and Lafayette were lovers.

Lalla had been working with Lafayette for about nine months when a tragedy occurred on the ninth day of May 1911 which was to have a major impact on Lalla's career. During a performance of "The Lion's Bride" at the Empire Theatre in Edinburgh[70], a fire broke out, killing ten people, including Lafayette. The lion also perished in the fire.

The story was reported extensively in the Scottish newspapers. A detailed account of events appeared in the *Aberdeen Journal* on the eleventh day of May. Following are extracts from the report:

One of the most disastrous conflagrations in the history of the country, involving the loss of nine lives, occurred, as stated in yesterday's issue, late on Tuesday night at the Empire Theatre of Varieties in Edinburgh. The outbreak occurred just about the close of the performances at the second house, and Lafayette, the great illusionist, one of the victims, was upon

---

[69] Liberace was an American pianist and entertainer who was at his peak from the 1950s to the 1970s. He had a flamboyant lifestyle and he was the highest paid entertainer of his time. He was homosexual although he denied it.
[70] Lalla had previously appeared at the Empire in the early days of her solo career in August 1904. George Formby senior was also on the bill. He was the father of George Formby, the famous British ukulele-playing music hall artist.

the stage. With startling suddenness, a great burst of flame rose from the scenery, and shot, by the force of the draught, across the auditorium. For a moment, the spectators formed the impression that the flames were a daring part of the performance. Presently, it was frightfully obvious that the stage was on fire. The fireproof curtain was immediately lowered, and the audience made their escape from the building in a comparatively orderly fashion. Meantime, horror reigned on the stage. The performers rushed from their dressing rooms and the stage hands fought the flames, but the fire spread so rapidly, and the heat was awful. Some of the artistes seem to have left the stage and returned. Lafayette was one of these, and it is thought that he had gone back to try to save his horse and dog. The body found in the left-hand corner of the stage beside the charred remains of the horse is supposed to be that of Lafayette [it was later identified by members of his company as his body]. The remains of the lion lay on the other side of the stage. At first it was supposed that no lives were lost, but subsequently, it was found that there were nine fatalities, six of the victims being members of Lafayette's company. Among the dead was C. Richards, a member of Lafayette's Company whose body has not yet been recovered. Five persons were admitted to the Royal Infirmary, but their injuries were not serious.

The report also gave some details of Lafayette's life:

Lafayette was an extremely wealthy man. He was one of the biggest American impresarios, and ran a number of his own companies in America. His company at Edinburgh numbered about thirty persons, and included "The Travesty Band", itself larger than Sousa's band[71]. His contract amounted to between £500 and £600 a week, and for the last ten years he is reported to have drawn about £40,000 a year. A teetotaller and a shrewd business man, he nevertheless possessed most eccentric habits. He was chiefly remarkable for his fondness for a Tennessee hound called "Beauty", to which he gave expression in a variety of strange ways[72]. He had a collar made for his dog studded with gold plates edged with diamonds, and in each of the plates was engraved a facsimile of the signature of the proprietor of the hall wherever he played. When these were filled, he bought the dog a gold curbed chain bracelet, and had the initials of other theatre proprietors stamped on the links. His house in Tavistock Square was decorated in his favourite colour – heliotrope [pink-purple] – and was filled with strange and wonderful things. A curious inscription in the house was the following: "You may sit at my table, you may drink my wine, you may give commands to my servants, but respect my dog". His opinion of this animal was so high that he affixed a motto outside the door: "The more I see of men, the more I love my dog". This, however, he is said to have been compelled to take down. Even his cheques were specially designed, being engraved with a portrait of the dog sitting by the side of bags of gold, and inscribed: "My two best friends". By a strange

---

[71] John Philip Sousa was a famous American composer and bandleader noted for military and patriotic marches.

[72] Lafayette was at his residence in Tavistock Square at the time of the 1911 census. He listed two persons at the house, himself and his sixteen year old "daughter" Beauty Lafayette! He stated that he was born in Los Angeles and he signed the schedule "The Great Lafayette". Under "infirmities", he entered "too quick" or possibly "too good". The entry is not very clear and it has been scored through by the enumerator.

coincidence, this dog died only last week, and Lafayette's grief at its death was well-nigh inconsolable.

The *Dundee Evening Telegraph* suggested that Lafayette's death was fate. It stated that that the loss of his dog so preyed upon his mind that he did not greatly care to outlive the animal. A story circulated that, on the death of Lafayette's sweetheart, he transferred all of his affection onto the dog, to which he was completely obsessed. He believed that the dog was his good luck mascot and, after it died, his luck ran out. The story is probably a myth, circulated after his death.

However, all was not as it seemed regarding his death. The body that had been identified as being Lafayette was taken to Glasgow to be cremated. Meanwhile, the search continued to find the body of the missing man, Charles Richards, and the searchers had almost given up hope, believing that the body had been crushed beyond recognition in the debris. However, Lafayette's London solicitor, Mr Alfred Nisbet, knew that Lafayette wore two valuable diamond rings and he raised doubts as to whether the body that had been found was indeed that of Lafayette. The search was intensified to try to find the rings. The rings were indeed found, together with a body. But it was not the body of Charles Richards, it was Lafayette! Of course, the discovery made headline news. The *Dundee Courier* carried the following report on the thirteenth day of May:

About half past five, one of the theatre staff named James Pattison, while searching in the debris under the stage, found a body lying face upwards under the opposite side of the stage. The body was lying with the arms partly extended over

185

the head, and although black and charred, the features were quite recognisable. Pattison left the body where he found it and brought down to see it one of Lafayette's company. Both men were at first under the impression that it was the body of the missing Richards, when the diamond rings which Lafayette wore were discovered on the fingers of the body. Mr Nesbit and Mr Samuel Lloyd, a great personal friend of Lafayette's, were summoned and when they arrived, they unhesitatingly confirmed the identification [of Lafayette].

Charles Richards had been employed by Lafayette as a "body double" which he used to create some of his illusions. Using a double enabled him to seem to appear in two different places in an instant. Ironically, the *Sunderland Daily Echo* reported the story under the headline: HIS LAST ILLUSION.

About the same time that Lafayette's body was discovered, the death toll from the fire rose to ten when one of the people hurt, James Neilson, died of his injuries at the Royal Infirmary.

Lafayette's funeral was as dramatic as his death. His brother, Alfred Neuberger, arrived from Paris and made a statement that he and Lafayette were born of American parents, in contradiction to the common belief that they were immigrants who took up American citizenship. It was planned to give Lafayette a Jewish burial but the local rabbi refused to perform the ceremony because Lafayette was to be buried in the same grave as his dog, Beauty. As a consequence, the funeral was led by a Presbyterian priest, the Reverend Finlay Clark.

Such was the public interest in Lafayette that tens of thousands of people lined the route of the funeral procession to the Piershill cemetery on the fourteenth day of May. Much public grief was displayed by some members of Lafayette's company and there were over fifty floral tributes that had arrived from all over the country. The principle mourners were Alfred Neuberger, Lafayette's brother, Alfred Nesbit, his London solicitor, Will Collins, his business manager, and his closest friends, Lalla Selbini, John Kirkamp, and Mr and Mrs Sam Lloyd. Lalla was supported by her mother, Lily Selbini [McCoy]. Lalla's floral tribute was especially noteworthy, as reported in the *Dundee Courier* the next day:

Lalla's floral tribute
The wreath in the shape of a dog was from Harry Houdini
(Courtesy of the "graveyard detective")

One wreath well merits notice. It was a proscenium of a theatre, worked in flowers, and stood six feet high. The uprights were of golden iris, and the drop scene of lily of the valley, with "The Last Act" worked in forget-me-knots. A little

187

note said simply, "To my dearly beloved lost friend, from Lalla Selbini."

Mademoiselle Selbini was the young lady who played the role of the lion's bride in the sketch of that name which was being produced on the fatal night. Her grief at the funeral was very evident.

Within twenty-four hours, films of the fire and the funeral were being shown in theatres throughout Britain and thousands of sightseers flocked to the cemetery to view Lafayette's grave.

"The Great Lalla Selbini"

Lalla Selbini, the only successor to The Great Lafayette
(Source: Vintage postcard)

On the nineteenth day of May 1911, the male members of Lafayette's company met and agreed to continue with their act under the leadership of three principle members; Messrs Jewitt, Williams, and Hughes. They obviously were not interested in the views of the female members! However, they were unsuccessful in establishing themselves as a viable act and they disbanded after only a few weeks.

Meanwhile, Lafayette's executors had granted Lalla Selbini exclusive rights to use any part of Lafayette's act. Less than two months later, Lalla re-launched her career by appearing at the Hippodrome Theatre in Sheffield and part of her act had her conducting Lafayette's Travesty Band. The original band had twenty members, some of whom lost their lives in the fire, and made up over half of Lafayette's company. The male members of the company who had met on the nineteenth day of May were perhaps a little relieved that the show had survived although I wonder how they felt about being led by a woman.

Lalla resurrected her "Bathing Beauty" act to complete the bill at the Hippodrome. I have not found any evidence that she continued to perform her act when she was working with Lafayette. She now included in her act some quick change routines, no doubt learned from Lafayette. Lalla would have been encouraged by the favourable review that she received:

Big houses enjoyed an excellent entertainment at the Hippodrome last night. The principle turn was provided by Lalla Selbini, who appeared with the late Lafayette's Travesty Band. The audience gave the band a hearty reception, but right through the performance, one felt that the master's hand was absent. Miss Selbini did well, especially when it is remembered that the entertainment is only just entering its second week, and the band gave her excellent support. In the first part of her show, Miss Selbini gave her turn, "The Bathing Beauty". She is a clever cyclist, and can do almost anything with a wheel. She also has a clever brother, who is a smart acrobat, and the pair give a pleasing dance. The whole entertainment was well received by the audience.

Lalla was a determined lady in a business that was dominated by male producers at that time. She resolved in the course of time to build up the whole Lafayette show as he had left it. On

190

the strength of Lafayette's reputation, Lalla was able to secure bookings in the United Kingdom for the next two years, after which she planned to take the act to America. By the end of 1911, she had included a "Teddy Bear" illusion into the act alongside her own act and that of the Travesty Band, which she conducted. And by June the following year, Lalla was performing almost the entire Lafayette repertoire, finishing the show with the "Lion's Bride" illusion, only, this time, Lalla played the Lafayette part rather than the part of the distressed damsel. But Lalla was a shrewd business woman and she understood the inherent dangers of performing the illusion. She hired two inventors, Frederick William Golby and John Selim Patterson, to make improvements to Lafayette's design of the lion's cage to ensure that the lion would never be able to have access to the actors at any time during the performance. Lalla applied for a patent for the device in May 1912 under her real name of Lalla Mary Pantzer.

Such a bold venture (to manage Lafayette's company) could have ended in disaster but Lalla had studied Lafayette at close quarters and she was able to imitate his mannerisms. And she was a big hit wherever she performed. The *Dundee Courier* reported on the eleventh day of June 1912 on her performance at the King's Theatre:

A week before he was due to appear at the King's Theatre, Dundee, The Great Lafayette met a tragic fate, and the music hall stage lost a mysterious and mighty personality. Lafayette is gone but there remains a rich heritage of brilliant spectacles in which he was the guiding hand. Lalla Selbini has stepped into the breach. A clever woman has succeeded a clever man. At the King's Theatre this week, Miss Selbini presents a selection of Lafayette's most famous productions, and last night she received a rousing welcome from two magnificent "houses". Lalla Selbini is remarkably versatile. When she first appears, it is to sing and dance most pleasingly, and to display clever cycling tricks. Thereafter, she enters with zest into the Lafayette programme, beginning with the humorous teddy bear illusion, which recalls a pathetic incident of the Edinburgh disaster. The travesty band was one of the best of Lafayette's enterprises. Good music and delightful comedy are splendidly combined by the instrumentalists, and the travesty band items were received with prolonged applause. The "Overture 1912" is thrilling. It is a revelation of the mind of Lafayette, with its mystery of light and turbulence of movement, the blare of trumpets, the cracking of pistols, and the roar of cannon. Lalla Selbini, in a general's uniform, comes upon the stage mounted on a charger, and the curtain falls upon a spectacular triumph. "The Lion's Bride" is the most elaborate of the illusions. It is a story of the Orient, worked out in an incense-laden harem. Upon a lion in a cage, the interest concentrates. The Prince (Lalla Selbini) falls in love with a slave girl, and the enraged Queen condemns the girl to the lion's den, and there she is left to her fate. She is not devoured by the lion but is rescued by the Prince in a lion's disguise. The real lion is no longer there, and the illusion is dexterously accomplished. Lalla Selbini and her company undoubtedly give a splendid entertainment.

In February 1913, Lalla took time out from performing to take a much-needed rest. She used the time to visit New York and to open up negotiations to take the Lafayette show to America. Martin Beck, the founder of the Orpheum Theatre circuit, wanted Lalla to open at the recently-opened Palace Theatre in New York on the fourteenth day of April and then to undertake a tour of the states but Lalla's demands for a weekly fee of $2500 was a stumbling block. *Variety Magazine* reported that Lalla had returned to England without a contract. However, Lalla recruited an agent, Jack York, to act on her behalf and he secured some bookings. She was back in America[73] with her company at the beginning of May, having been booked to appear at the Bijou Theatre in Orange County, New Jersey. Lalla possibly had to agree on a lower fee than that she had originally demanded.

When the show arrived in Orange County, the lion that she used in the "Lion's Bride" illusion was caged in a railroad car while her scenery was removed to the theatre. Two boys thought that it would be a good prank to release the lion! Of course, panic ensued and all attempts to capture the wild beast were fruitless. The local patrolman tried to shoot the lion from a long distance but, fortunately for the show and the lion, he failed. Finally, a local cowboy, Joe Amento, managed to lasso the lion but before he was able to take any further, possibly terminal, action, Lalla arrived at the scene. She called out the lion's name and led him away like a tame pet. The *New York Times* reported:

---

[73] It is possible that Lalla remained in America and did not return to England.

193

Mme Lalla walked right up to the captive [lion] and produced a sensation by loosening the rope and indignantly casting it off. "Why, Pete, what have they been doing to you?" she asked, patting the beast comfortingly for, by this time, Pete was feeling dejected. "Come along with me". Pete followed Mme Lalla to his freight car, and to the cheers of the assembled multitude, hopped nimbly into his cage. Apparently, he was more relieved than anyone else when the cage door was again closed. How it ever came open is the only element of mystery in the adventure.

Cynically, one may think that the escape was set up to create publicity for the show but would Lalla have risked the lion's life with such a stunt?

The company appeared next at Keith's Union Square Theatre on Broadway for the week commencing the eighteenth day of May and Lalla was billed as "The Great Lalla Selbini, the only successor to The Great Lafayette". Sime Silverman of *Variety Magazine* reviewed her show but he was a little unsure about its future because of the cost of staging it:

The name of the Great Lafayette might be perpetuated in vaudeville by Lalla Selbini (now with "the Great" tagged on) who is employing all the late and great showman's variety material in the two turns she is presenting at the Union Square this week. Miss Selbini, according to the general understanding, is making use of this property, effects, illusions, comedy, and acts by right. The final act is "the Lion's Bride". Miss Selbini does her best work with it. The illusion seems to have been newly built, except the lion perhaps. It is well put on, has strength and force, runs quickly in the manner Lafayette formerly worked it, and carries a horse, also a prop elephant. *"The Lion's Bride"* as shown by Carter, the Magician, at the Fifth Avenue a few weeks ago is a weakling alongside the Selbini production although Carter used a Lafayette copy, but whether he did so by right or not is unknown. The first act Selbini did was composed of some of Lafayette's tricks, his comedy band (12 pieces), and *"The Great Fire Drama"*, claimed by the programme to be Lalla's own. It has a spectacular effect for the finale; that of a fire engine coming head on to the audience. Three prop horses are driven by two men and a girl. Light effects could accomplish something with it. Miss Selbini opens this part with her former single speciality of trick bicycle riding in a bathing (union) suit. She still retains her girlish figure and still isn't a bit afraid to show it all. Miss Selbini also sings one of her songs. It is called *"Hello, Hello, My Little Mermaid"* and is an English number, but Selbini's voice has not been trained for stage singing. She is the barber in the Strauss waltz, which Lafayette made so humorous, [and which] has been extensively pilfered. For this, Selbini uses an ordinary chair, very likely because her height does not permit the employment of a regular barber's chair. The latter would greatly strengthen this portion. The band is more noisy than musical. Other numbers with the musicians are *"Wee MacGregor"* with Selbini costumed as a Scotchman while leading; *"Herr Katzenstein"*, the Svengali number with Miss Selbini as the German, conducting for a young woman who sings, and *"The Japanese Teddy Bear Wonder"*, a light bit of magic. (*"Leda and the Swan"*, programmed but not given). Selbini takes care of *"the Lion's Bride"* nicely and has played up to a point or so beyond where it was when Lafayette left

195

this country to meet his death in Glasgow. [He died in Edinburgh]. But the early portion apparently requires even yet the showmanship Lafayette always interjected into everything he did. Lalla is somewhat deficient in this regard, mostly because she is a woman, but the girl works sincerely and very hard all the time. The audience takes to her. She has a chance of getting these acts across over here. The trouble may arise on bookings through terms offered and demanded. If Miss Selbini has acquired the right to the name of The Great Lafayette, she should use it, not for the commercial value it may have, but out of respect for one of the great showmen who ever appeared on a vaudeville stage and a man who had spirit, with the courage to back that up, and a man who made himself in the show business.

Perhaps it was a little naive of the reviewer to suggest that Lalla should continue with Lafayette's show without suitable recompense. After all, she would have to pay the members of the ensemble and the costs of transporting the show across America would have been high. However, Lalla was unable to secure bookings on her terms and she took a big gamble. Through her agent, Jack York, she negotiated a deal with the manager of the Liberty Theatre in Philadelphia to appear on "shared terms". I believe that this agreement meant that, after costs, Lalla and the theatre shared the profits, if any. The experiment proved to be a great success:

The Alhambra surprised everyone in town by landing a big act for the week, for the first time in Philadelphia. This is the Lalla Selbini production of the Great Lafayette Show, with a score of people and enough paraphernalia to fill a sixty-foot baggage car. The show is unique, pleasing, and one of the

196

biggest acts ever produced in a ten-and-twenty-cent theatre.
Manager Frank Migone took a chance on the week with such
a big production, but that it will prove profitable is proven by
the turn-a-way business of yesterday.

Lalla quickly secured another engagement in Philadelphia the following week at the Keystone Theatre but obtaining further bookings proved to be difficult. She had to settle for a contract with Jones, Linick and Schaeffer of Chicago for an eight week engagement to appear as the big feature on their small time circuit and she opened at the Colonial Theatre in Chicago on the eleventh day of August. The appearance at the Colonial was a disaster. Lalla fainted twice during her performance and she was obviously unwell, whether due to exhaustion or due to a virus is unknown. Consequently, she gave a poor performance and she was slated by the critics:

Lalla Selbini was last week's feature at the Colonial
presenting three different acts – bicycle, travesty band, and
the Lion's Bride. This is a very ambitious attempt on her part
and the act has been described in these words: 'Mediocrity
never made such a flash'. Miss Selbini has a poor voice for
either singing or talking and her company seems to have been
gathered together with the idea of holding down expenses.

As a consequence of the appearance, Jones, Linick and Schaefer cancelled the contract and it was reported that Lalla put her equipment into storage, pending litigation. Whether she proceeded with the litigation is unknown but Lalla and her company soon found more work. They appeared at the Talbot Hippodrome Theatre in St Louis the following week so it is debatable whether the equipment actually ever went into

197

storage! The show was a big success and Lalla was immediately booked to appear at the Talbot Hippodrome Theatre in Kansas City. However, further bookings continued to prove difficult and it is doubtful that Lalla was able to recoup her costs. She soldiered on for the next six months but she probably became disillusioned with the tour and she abandoned her plan to lead the company. Within a year, the company had been disbanded and Lalla returned to her solo career.

Lalla Re-Launches Her Solo Career

After the disbandment of Lafayette's Company, Lalla stayed in America. It would seem that she remained a favourite with the Hammerstein family and she was signed by Willie Hammerstein for the Victoria Roof Garden for the week of the fifth day of May 1914 to appear in her old act – the bicycle riding speciality. After a week's absence from the Hammerstein programme, she returned in June, billed as *"The Girl With The Most Beautiful Eyelashes In The World"*. In addition to her established bicycle act, she wore French false eyelashes. Sime Silverman in *Variety* wrote his usual negative review of Lalla's act:

Another bathing suit, a union suit in fact, enclosed another "single", Lalla Selbini, "The girl with the most beautiful eyelashes in the world". Yes? Lalla is cheating the boys, although at the matinees this week, Lionel Haskell is piloting Lalla through the orchestra, she carrying a hand electric to flash upon those French made lashes that are sold by the piece or pound in Paris. At night, Lalla and her union suit become the attraction on "The Farm" at intermission, she riding about on a bicycle while the crowd divides its attention between her lashes and her legs, as Lalla's union suit is disfigured by a silver girdle and a stretch of bare flesh. Mr Haskell made a hit of the act in the afternoon Monday with comment on Lalla and her lashes as the couple patrolled up and down the aisle. "The most beautiful, etc" was hardly enough to have warranted the bicycle rider a return date so quickly at Hammerstein's. She isn't carrying around a good facial makeup and for her "single" turn, Lalla really needs something more than she has at present.

199

Whether the use of the eyelashes was simply a ploy adopted by Lalla to obtain publicity is open to debate but she soon abandoned the gimmick. And she did indeed get more work when she joined Jean Bedini's "Mischief Makers" show although her time with the show was short-lived. The show opened to poor audiences at the Chicago American Music Hall and its format was quickly revised. Lalla was a casualty of the revision and she left the show before it went on tour. She continued to perform as a solo artist, being billed as the "Venus on Wheels" although she was finding it difficult to get engagements and she was no longer a star billing. According to the *New York Clipper*, Lalla planned to return to England in April 1917 to undertake an engagement but, in February, she joined Sarah Bernhardt's Vaudeville Road Show instead, playing at theatres in Brooklyn, Boston, New England, and Canada.

America entered the First World War in April 1917 and the worldwide influenza epidemic began to spread later in the same year. The epidemic meant that a number of performers were unable to work and Lalla took the opportunity to support the war effort by placing the following advertisement in the newspapers:

Women of the Stage!
LALLA SELBINI
REQUESTS

that the women of the stage now obliged to lay off through the epidemic

DO HOSPITAL or RED CROSS WORK
It Kills Time and Helps to Kill Huns

It is not known if Lalla took her own advice!

On completion of the tour with Sarah Bernhardt's show, Lalla played at the Fifth Avenue Theatre in New York in August 1917. The *New York Clipper* reported on her (new) act in some detail:

Lalla Selbini will be recalled for her burlesque and vaudeville reputation of a few years ago. She has returned to vaudeville with a rather novel offering which, at present, however, is a bit crude. Miss Selbini opens in one, singing a French song, and dances her way into full stage as the curtain arises at the end of the number. She then mounts a bicycle and, after shedding her soubrette dress, displays as attractive a form as she did in years gone by. She does several poses while riding on the wheel which are quite impressive. However, during this work it might be advisable for her to eliminate the talk she uses, as it is too typical of burlesque and only appeals to that element of an audience. With this work, she has a male assistant who does a bit of comedy work that is entirely out of place. Miss Selbini follows this with a drawing on a trick blackboard. She draws the picture of a dog and then the assistant places a cover over the board. When it is taken off, a live dog is revealed. The woman then rides around the stage on a wagon wheel, with the dog running between the spokes. She also does several posing stunts, riding on the handle bars of the machine, after which she rides around on a single wheel dressed in a Hawaiian costume and playing the ukulele. For an encore she does a bit of a dance rather reminiscent of burlesque. The act, if curtailed in a few spots, especially at the finish, would make an acceptable opening or closing offering.

However, her performance was savaged by *Variety Magazine* (the article was probably written by Sime Silverman, who hardly ever gave Lalla any credit for her talent):

After Pictorial Weekly Review came Lalla Selbini, the once famous cycling beauty. In lemon coloured silk with large blackbirds appliquéd on the short skirt, and white shoes and tights, she danced and sang, first in English then in French. Astride her wheel she made a quick change to a white silk one piece negligee, so thin you could see her flesh through it. For her closing unicycle stunt she wore an over-trimmed Hawaiian dress. Miss Selbini's indifferent manner, untidy hair, etc, easily explain why she is no longer a feature act.

In spite of the poor review, Lalla continued to get bookings across America based on her "bathing beauty" act, although she was fast-approaching her fortieth birthday. However, her costumes were now more befitting her age. A good description of them appeared in Variety Magazine when it reviewed her performance at the Lincoln Theatre in New York in April 1919:

A Chinese coat and pants of white satin trimmed with blue and a bonnet of graduate rows of pearls was somewhat out of the ordinary for a cycling costume, and most effective. She makes her changes on the stage and strips to a turquoise blue union suit. Miss Selbini, who was at one time considered the prettiest girl on the English Music Hall stage, and is still pretty, for that matter, was undoubtedly the first to adopt this daring attire for bicycle riding.

202

Lalla was still able to put on a satisfactory performance. When she appeared at Greeley Square in New York, one newspaper reported, somewhat briefly:

Miss Selbini hopped in a couple of times, with her tights, riding a wheel. Miss Selbini can still ride a wheel and wear tights.

In a change of direction, Lalla joined the cast of "Happy Days", produced by Charles Dillingham with music by Raymond Hubbell, which opened at the New York Hippodrome in August 1919. The show was a huge musical extravaganza in three acts and had a cast of over one thousand artists, the vast majority of whom were employed in supporting roles such as musicians and chorus lines. There were three hundred chorus girls. Lalla appeared in the first act in a scene called "Fairyland" and in the second act in a scene called "A Chinese Cabaret Restaurant". She performed her speciality act on a bicycle and she retained her popularity with the public. The Prince of Wales, later King Edward VIII, attended the show on the twenty-first day of November 1919. The show became the first one to break the $100,000 weekly takings for a show on Broadway. It ran for nine months, performing 452 times, and when it closed, Lalla began another, and final, phase of her long career in show business.

Lalla, (centre) in "Happy Days"
with Belle Story and Arthur Geary
(Source: The Sun. (New York [N.Y.]), 30 Nov. 1919. Chronicling America:
Historic American Newspapers)

Lalla and Bert Nagle

Bert Nagle was born Adelbert Jacob Nagle on the fourth day of September 1896[74] in Bangor, Pennsylvania, the son of Amelius Nagle. He was drafted into the US Army on the first day of May 1918 during the First World War but, fortunately [for him], he did not serve overseas and he was discharged on the first day of July 1919. Prior to joining the army, he was a carpenter but he entered show business immediately after his release. He was of small stature, standing just five feet and three inches tall. He was supposedly a protégé of Irvin Berlin.

Bert Nagle from his passport application in 1924
(Courtesy of Ancestry.co.uk)

"Happy Days" was probably his first appearance on the stage. He appeared in the first scene of the first act of "Happy Days", playing the part of Mr Calico, a visitor, in a scene called "The Kiddies' Dormitory". He and Lalla became acquainted and, after the Broadway run of the show, they created their own original sketch entitled "The Butterfly and the Cat" in which Lalla continued to perform her trick cycling

---

[74] Some records give his year of birth as 1894 or 1895. His army record, which is probably the most reliable, gives his birth year as 1896.

and juggling and Bert provided the comedy dressed as a cat. Bert claimed a record for speed in travelling on all fours. In June 1920, Lalla announced that, in future, her billing will be *Selbini and Nagle* although, on a number of advertisements, Lalla and Bert were billed as *Selbini and Albert*. The act made its debut on Fifth Avenue in September 1920 and it received a favourable report in *Variety Magazine*:

This looks like a new frame-up for Miss Selbini and she certainly is packing a lot of variety into nine minutes of time that she and her partner occupy the stage. The act is opened by Miss Selbini playing the violin. The partner, who appears as a cat throughout the act, responds to her calls for a little comedy scene in one. In full stage, he works with the little bike rider in a series of acrobatic leaps and fills in the picture while she is dancing and riding. For the greater part of the act, Miss Selbini works in trousered garb of a flowered material, but for her final bit, she strips down to the famous blue and white union suit and does some riding on a bike camouflaged as a butterfly; pretty concept and effective for stage purposes. The act can open or close in the big houses and fill in, in almost any spot on a small big time show.

Lalla had retained her natural beauty and the New York Herald stated in their review that:

It was a delightful cycling and singing act. Miss Selbini is rightly called "the most perfect woman in vaudeville"

Lalla and Bert soon secured a contract to appear on the Orpheum Circuit of Vaudeville theatres across provincial America and Canada. The theatres were more "big time" than some of the theatres that Lalla had appeared in after she disbanded the Lafayette Company. The act was well-received and Lalla and Bert were encouraged to continue with it after they had completed the Orpheum tour. They spent the following year performing in Great Britain, arriving in Southampton on board the passenger ship *Mauritania* on the twenty-second day of July 1921. Bert was recorded as Jacob Nagle and Lalla was recorded as Mary McCoy in the passenger list. Bert stated on a later passport application that they had played in England, Scotland, Wales, and Ireland. They returned to New York in 1922, embarking on board the passenger ship *SS Aquitania* on the twenty-fourth day of June and arriving in New York on the first day of July.

In July 1922, Lalla and Bert appeared again on Broadway. Their act had been modified a little since they last appeared in New York in 1920. For once, *Variety Magazine* gave her a favourable review. For some strange reason, the reviewer, not Sime Silverman this time, thought that Bert was a female! However, since Bert was not much taller than Lalla who was petite, the mistake was perhaps understandable.

Miss Selbini is back after a long while abroad. In her new turn, she is assisted by Bert Nagel (sic) an animal actress. Nagel, as a cat, capers about the stage, taking some remarkable falls and leaps from table to table, covering a tremendous distance. She also does a dive through paper hoops held by Miss Selbini. The turn opens in "one" with a song by the girl [Lalla] to her own violin accompaniment. This introduces the cat impersonator who gets attention immediately with her loose-jointed contortions. The turn goes to full stage. Miss Selbini, after a change to shorter skirts, flashes a graceful soft shoe buck dance, followed by bicycle

207

riding. The cat entertains with some funny pantomime, trying to catch a prop spider while the girl makes another change to her famous one-piece costume. Mounted atop a bicycle with a special "dragonfly" body, Miss Selbini attired in a one-piece costume with a white bodice, makes a pretty picture beneath changing coloured lights as she rides about the stage in different poses. At the finish, the cat, with illuminated eyes, dashes around her in a circle. It's a real novelty and should be in demand for the best of the bills. Miss Selbini is a picture in all of her costumes and hasn't lost any of her versatility. Nagel is a strong comedy addition.

Lalla and Bert continued touring America for the next two years, after which they undertook another brief tour of England. They arrived in Southampton on the eighth day of August 1924 and they made appearances in Bristol, London and Exeter, where they were received favourably. The review of their performance at the Bristol Hippodrome in the *Western Daily Press* on the twenty-third day of September 1924 reported:

Some very breezy fooling was provided by Lalla Selbini and Bert Albert in "The Cat and the Butterfly", a scenelet introducing a variety of elements. The former did some clever trick bicycle riding, and the latter made an incomparable Felix.

Lalla and Bert returned to America at the beginning of 1925 although they did not travel together. Bert arrived aboard the passenger ship *SS Berengaria* which arrived in New York on the fourth day of February 1925 but Lalla did not arrive in New York until two weeks' later. She had stayed in England a little longer to visit her parents and daughter who were living in Clacton-on-Sea in the county of Essex at that time.

Lalla and Bert resumed touring America and Canada for the next three years. Their appearances included theatres in San Francisco, Toronto, Montreal, London, Peoria (Illinois), Chester (Pennsylvania), New York, Harrisburg (Pennsylvania), Boston, Little Rock (Arkansas), and Birmingham (Alabama). By early 1928, the act had probably reached the end of its useful life. Lalla was approaching her fiftieth birthday and Bert probably wanted to progress onto other things. The partnership was dissolved and an announcement was placed in *Variety Magazine* in May 1928:

Bert Nagle, formerly Bert Albert of Lalla Selbini and Albert, an international act for eight years since R. H. Burnside's "Happy Days" show at the New York Hippodrome, now playing the comedy "Felix the Cat", in R. H. Burnside's first public unit at the Paramount, New York in "Kat Kabaret".

Lalla retired from show business[75] and Bert made a career out of performing as a cat for the next thirty years. Indeed, in the 1950s, he appeared on television in Walt Disney's *Mickey Mouse Club* as a cat. Bert died in his home town of Bangor on the twenty-second day of December 1962.

---

[75] I have not found any references to Lalla performing after May 1928 although she may have appeared with Archie Royer's circus.

The End of a Career

Lalla settled in America. She was able to claim American citizenship through her marriage to Willy Pantzer who, ironically, abandoned America and took up British citizenship. She had maintained contact with her family throughout her adult career and when she retired, she moved next door to her sister Mizpah and her husband, Archie Royer, in Geneva in Van Buren County in Michigan. In the 1930 census, Lalla was listed as Mary E Pantzer, a single woman, aged forty-four years, and with no occupation. She was living alone. A few years later, she moved six miles away to Bangor, presumably to a better house, but she was still living close to her sister.

In 1937, Lalla journeyed to England to visit her daughter, Patricia, and her husband and she arrived in Southampton on board the *SS Aquitania* on the tenth day of August. Patricia had married Ernest Lewis in Wandsworth in 1935 and they lived at 8 Leaf Grove, West Norwood, in London. I have not found any evidence that Ernest and Patricia had any children. Lalla stayed in England for five months, celebrating Christmas with her daughter and she arrived back in New York on the eleventh day of January 1938.

Her entry in the 1940 census gave her age as forty-eight years so she apparently had only aged four years in the last ten years! She was still living on her own.

Lalla suffered a stroke at her home in Bangor on the ninth day of February 1942 and she died two days later. The local newspaper, *The News-Palladium*, published her obituary on the twelfth day of February 1942[76]:

LALLA PANTZER, ENGLISH DANCER, DIES AT BANGOR
Lalla Mary Pantzer, a professional entertainer most of her life, died last evening at her home here following a stroke suffered Monday. With her parents, Patrick and Lillian McCoy, she played before many of the royal families in Europe, using as her stage name, Lalla Selbini. She was born 50 years ago in London, England[77]. Besides her dancing ability she was a talented musician and worked as an instructor for a number of years. Surviving is a daughter, Mrs. Patricia Lalla Lewis, in London; two sisters, Mrs. Leola Harraway, of Kingston, Ontario, Canada, and Mrs. Mizpah Royer, of Bangor, whose husband, Archie, has retired from connections with one of the larger circuses. Funeral services will be held in the Sacred Heart church, with the time of services not definite.

The funeral service was subsequently set for Saturday, the fourteenth day of February at 10:45 a.m. Of course, Lalla was in fact sixty-three years old but she was always secretive about her age! Presumably, she worked as a music instructor during her retirement years although in both the 1930 and 1940 censuses, it was stated that she had no earnings. Perhaps she provided the music lessons for free or she was avoiding having to pay any tax!

Lalla was buried in Monks Cemetery in Bangor in plot 63 on the fourteenth day of February 1942. She possibly left a will but there are no probate records for her at the Van Buren County Probate Court. Her death was registered under the

---

[76] Reproduced, courtesy of *The Herald-Palladium, Michigan.*
[77] Lalla was born on the Isle of Man in 1878.

name of Lalla Mary Pantzear (sic), the daughter of Patrick Joseph McCoy and Lillian Knight.

Another obituary for Lalla appeared in *Billboard Magazine* on the twenty-eighth day of February 1942:

SELBINI, Lalla (Mrs Mary Pantzer), 63, former cyclist and member of the third generation of English vaude[ville] family, February 11 in Bangor, MI. She was teamed with Bert Nagle until her retirement 12 years ago. She was the widow of Willie Pantzer of the Pantzer Brothers, well-known vaude[ville] act many years ago. She leaves a daughter and three sisters.

The report got her age correct but she only had two sisters, Leola and Mizpah. And, of course, she was not the widow of Willy Pantzer. He was still living and they had divorced in 1909.

Lalla's modest gravestone
(Courtesy of "Scout" at findagrave.com)

Lalla: A Retrospective

Lalla had a career in show business for over forty-five years, which she was able to sustain by her natural beauty and her cycling and juggling skills, although at times, her skills were not always appreciated by some theatre critics, especially in America, who were more obsessed with the way that she looked rather than what she did. She remained a favourite with audiences throughout her career. Of course, her appearance was something that Lalla exploited; firstly and successfully as "the bathing beauty", and afterwards less successfully as "the girl with the most beautiful eyelashes in the world". Whether it was Lalla's idea or the idea of the theatre managers, Lalla's nationality when stated, was billed as French, American or English to enhance her appeal to the audiences. Of course, she was British, born on the Isle of Man.

Did Lalla have ambitions to be a singer? Female singers were among the highest paid performers on the stage in the early 1900s but Lalla's voice was considered too weak to have any great success as a singer. She included [long-forgotten] light-hearted songs in her act such as "Mariutch Down at Coney Isle" and "Bonjour, Marie", and she even wrote some items, such as "Hello, Hello, My Little Mermaid". Another song that Lalla may have performed in her act was "My Fluff a De Ruff". Published in 1908, the music was written by James Brockman and Ed Gardiner wrote the lyrics. Lalla's picture was used on the cover of the sheet music but the song was clearly written for a male performer. The song was recorded by Ed Morton, an American comic baritone, in 1908.

What about Lalla's relationships with men? Apart from her father, there were only three notable ones. When she married Willy Pantzer, the couple seemed well-suited but it became evident that Willy wanted to control Lalla's career, which she naturally resisted. The fall-out from the "Dainty Duchess" contract eventually caused the marriage to break up and the split seems to have perhaps affected Lalla's attitude towards men more than she may have cared to admit. She never remarried and she dedicated her life to her show business career. Although she used *Lalla Selbini* as her stage name, she used her maiden name of *Mary McCoy* on a number of occasions when she travelled. Formally, she remained *Mrs Mary Pantzer* up to the time of her death.

Lalla's relationship with The Great Lafayette is interesting. When they first met in New York, Lafayette acted as Lalla's mentor. It was probably Lalla's discontent with the "Dainty Duchess" contract that brought them together. Lafayette was a very successful showman and, maybe, Lalla aspired to similar fame. She could not discuss her concerns with Willy and, perhaps, Lafayette saw the same ambition for success in Lalla that he himself possessed. In spite of rumours, it is unlikely that Lalla and Lafayette's relationship was more than platonic. Had it been anything more, Lalla would probably have joined Lafayette's company much sooner than she did. Indeed, she only teamed up with him four years later in 1910. In a short time, Lalla was able to understand how Lafayette performed many of his illusions and how he managed his company which enabled her to take control of it after his death. Whether Lafayette "taught" Lalla or whether she picked up the knowledge through observation is open to speculation.

Certainly, Lafayette was a very private man although he was not unsociable. Lalla's floral tribute to Lafayette at his funeral suggests that they had a very close professional friendship.

In addition to his favourite pet, Beauty, Lafayette had other animals in his act which he also doted on. It was believed that he re-entered the fire at the Embassy Theatre in Edinburgh to save his horse. One of his pet dogs, Fifi, survived the fire and Lalla cared for her and probably used her in her cycling act. When Fifi died in 1917, Lalla gave the animal a grand "send off" in true Lafayette style:

LAFAYETTE'S "FIFI" DIES; Roanoke, VA, Nov 21 1917
"Fifi", once the favourite pet fox terrier of the late Great Lafayette, died here yesterday and was accorded a royal funeral by Lalla Selbini, who owned the animal. She has had him embalmed and buried in a specially built casket. "Fifi" worked in one of Lafayette's illusions.

Lalla's third relationship was with Bert Nagle. When they met, she was forty years old and he was twenty-three years old and new to show business. At the time, Lalla was looking for a new direction in her career and she and Bert were very successful with "The Butterfly and the Cat". Was the relationship between Lalla and Bert purely professional or was there more to it? Lalla was still considered a very attractive woman who had lost none of her natural beauty so it is possible that Bert found her alluring. Marriage between them would possibly not have been an option given the age difference. However, there are no reports in the newspaper of their social life and it may be, of course, that Lalla simply saw potential in Bert and wished to develop his career, while helping her to enhance her own career. During their partnership, Bert lived with his married sister, Florence Foulks, in Long Island so it is more likely that his relationship with Lalla was purely professional.

Lalla was clearly a strong-willed woman and she did not rely on others to manage her career, although Willy certainly tried to do so. As early as 1908, "The Actors' Yearbook" stated *Lalla Selbini is a worthy exponent of the modern-day woman of brains and ambition.* After her split from Willy, Lalla took control of her own affairs but not always without problems, as illustrated by the litigation that she was involved in. She personally entered into contract negotiations but she still had to rely on an agent to secure theatre bookings. She showed her independence in the way that she took control of Lafayette's show after his death and in her creation of "The Butterfly and the Cat".

Throughout her adult career, Lalla kept in close contact with her family. Her favourite seems to have been her sister Mizpah who accompanied her on her tour of Europe in 1908. And, of course, Lalla and Mizpah were both touring America in the 1910s when their paths must have crossed many times.

However, Lalla's relationship with her daughter Patricia is unclear. Soon after Patricia's birth, Lalla went to South Africa. After a brief return to England, she went to America so Patricia would not have seen much of her mother during her formative years. As soon as she was old enough, Patricia was sent to boarding school and she attended St Joseph's Convent and Boarding School in Hendon, Middlesex. As an adult, she lived with her grandparents, Jack and Lily Selbini in

Melfort Road, Thornton Heath, until she married Ernest Lewis in 1935. Perhaps Lalla's visit in 1937 was an attempt to make up for lost time.

In retirement, Lalla kept a low profile, living alone but close to her sister Mizpah. She owned the houses in Bangor that she lived in so, presumably, she had invested sufficient money from her earnings, which had been substantial, to make such purchases and to provide herself with an annuity. In 1922, Lalla applied for the issue of a new Land Certificate for a property in Wandsworth to replace one that had been lost or destroyed. At that time, her address was given as Stockwell Park Road, Brixton although she was then resident in America. I assume that she also owned the Brixton house which was quite substantial, having eight rooms.

Lalla was clearly a beautiful woman who had demonstrated a variety of skills throughout her show business career, which enabled her at various times to be a trick cyclist, dancer, musician, singer, actress, comedienne and illusionist. Perhaps the only surprise is that she never appeared in any motion pictures. She was obviously photogenic and she had played light-hearted roles on the stage but, perhaps, she was unable to make the transition to movies. Or, perhaps, she never had any offers to appear on film, although personally I find that hard to believe. We will never know!

LALLA SELBINI WAS A REMARKABLE LADY

Appendix – Changes from First Edition

This appendix is only meaningful if you have read the first edition.

A number of amendments have been made since the first edition to correct some errors and to provide more details. In summary, these changes are:

- The surname of Mary Dorthy, wife of John Chatters, is likely to have been Doherty.
- Jeffery Hertford, John's nephew, should be John Hertford (or Hartford).
- Details are provided on the deaths of John's son, John, and his wife Sarah.
- Kate and William Knight had two more children, Catherine Mary and James, who died as infants.
- The dates of birth are identified for Kate and William's other children, Agnes and William.
- At the time of her death, I speculated that she was estranged from her husband and that she may have abandoned her children. That claim is incorrect.
- The date of birth of Lily Selbini (Knight) is confirmed.
- More details are given of William Knight's (son of Kate) career after the death of Frank Elton. I have also identified the name of his wife and the date of his death in Lambeth.
- There are significant changes to the chapter *The Selbinis – Swan Song* as more evidence has become available from the newspapers of the time.
- I have confirmed that Leola continued performing with the Selbini troupe until she married in 1912.
- The assumption that Victor played a poodle on pantomime is incorrect. The poodle was played by Ernest Selbini (stage name) who joined the troupe after William Selbini left.

- More details are provided on the career of Victor after the troupe disbanded in 1918. He continued in show business performing a bicycle act with his wife.
- I have added a new section to the chapter *The Selbinis – The Legacy* which summarises other individuals who appeared with the act at some time.
- Details are given of the marriage between Lalla Selbini and Willy Pantzer.
- I have found evidence that Willy Pantzer returned to America with his troupe of midgets in the 1920s but I still have not found evidence that they performed there.

11002612R00119

Printed in Great Britain
by Amazon